MOLLY'S
Amazing Grace

MOLLY'S
Amazing Grace

The remarkable true story of selfless love
and surrender triumphing over great trials

Tim Frink *and* Molly Frink

XULON PRESS

Xulon Press
2301 Lucien Way #415
Maitland, FL 32751
407.339.4217
www.xulonpress.com

Printed in the United States of America

Paperback ISBN-13: 978-1-6628-1686-4
Ebook ISBN-13: 978-1-6628-1687-1

❄ ❄ ❄

This book is dedicated to my amazing wife, Molly Frink,
who taught me, her family, friends, and students
how to follow Jesus and put the Father on display.
*You showed us day by day how to lay your life down for
those you love.*

AMAZING GRACE

Amazing grace! How sweet the sound
That saved a wretch like me!
I once was lost, but now am found;
Was blind, but now I see.

'Twas grace that taught my heart to fear,
And grace my fears relieved;
How precious did that grace appear
The hour I first believed.

Through many dangers, toils, and snares,
I have already come;
'Tis grace hath brought me safe thus far,
And grace will lead me home.

When we've been there ten thousand years,
Bright shining as the sun,
We've no less days to sing God's praise
Than when we first begun.

—John Newton, 1779

ACKNOWLEDGMENTS

We want to thank Joie Samuelson, Allison McGolrick, and Jan Winey for your great help editing this book. Your insights and suggestions were invaluable in helping us make our story come alive. We greatly appreciate our many friends who helped us tell our story. We treasure the loving friendship of our dear friends Jane Madjeski, Linnea Rawlins, Bob Guild, and Russ Miller. Your devotion, support, and encouragement helped sustain us on our long journey of faith.

Writing a book is like having a baby.
It is one of the most painful experiences of your life
but also one of the richest and most satisfying.

Introduction:

A LIFE OF LOVE

*M*olly grew up on a farm in rural Pennsylvania in the 1950s. Though her family would be considered impoverished by today's standards, they were rich beyond measure with a large, loving family and many nearby relatives. She grew up, went to college, got married, and had a lovely family. Everything was great, with the fulfillment of all her expectations for a wonderful middle-class life virtually in sight. But then, everything changed.

In this remarkable true story, Molly, with Tim, her husband, will share many stories of the Lord's faithfulness through the great trials in their lives. They repeatedly learned that His grace was truly sufficient in every crisis, even in the valley of the shadow of death. Throughout the book, friends and family members will also share stories and insights about how Molly profoundly impacted their lives.

You will see how Molly learned how to lay her life down and serve others as she abandoned herself to God, regardless of great pain and suffering. Through every trial, she developed such an expectancy in Jesus, knowing that He, like He always does, would work everything out for good.

Author Hannah Hurnard, best known for her timeless allegory *Hinds' Feet on High Places*, gives us the secret behind the powerful love and the amazing grace that was so readily apparent in Molly's life:

The secret of experiencing true love is:
To go lower.
    Pour yourself down.
      Go lower
        And lower.
Give and give and give,
    And serve with
      Joyful abandonment.

Molly poured herself into the lives of family members, friends, and students. She kept giving of her time and her talents everywhere she could and loved everyone in her plain, simple way. She considered herself just an ordinary woman who joyfully abandoned herself for everyone the Lord brought into her life. Hopefully, this book will inspire the reader to strive to live the theme song of her life: "It Is All About Love."

CONTENTS

1

THE ACCIDENT—
MOLLY'S STORY

*M*y life changed forever on Christmas Eve 1986. My children and I had just left the church when we were struck from the rear by a drunk driver. Rescue workers took me and my sons, Andy, thirteen, and Nate, eleven, to St. Mary's Hospital. But my precious Katie, age six, was taken by ambulance and then by helicopter to Children's Hospital Washington, D.C., with a severe closed head injury. Doctors gave her only a 30 percent chance of survival.

We were treated and released, and Pastor Lanny took us home. His love wrapped us safe and warm on a dismal night filled with pain and anxious prayers. I spent a restless night wrestling with God and pleading for the life of my little girl. Lanny took me to Children's Hospital on Christmas Day, and we sat and prayed and cried all day long. Soon, fellow believers in dozens of churches were interceding before the Lord on Katie's behalf. Hundreds of family and friends joined in prayers for her survival. The intracranial pressure, indicating severe damage, was dangerously high. It was twenty-five when Katie was admitted and should have been only four. Throughout the long hard day, we watched the monitor, which showed intracranial pressures anywhere between thirteen and eighteen. Lanny was a rock of support and encouragement in my very hard place. He said he thought the Lord wanted him to pray for ten, and we rejoiced as we saw it go down to eight before he finally left late that night.

Praise God—she survived the night, thanks to the mercy of the Lord and the prayers of the saints! The next day a friend brought a calendar with daily verses, and I rejoiced: "Behold I make all things new" (Rev. 21:5 NKJV).

I clung to this promise and repeated it for months and years to come.

For the next several months, I divided my time between two boys at home and my precious daughter fighting for her life in the hospital. Every Monday, the boys would go to school and then stay with friends while I spent the week in the hospital with Katie. I would come home every Saturday to spend a couple of days with the boys. Katie was unconscious for weeks while I prayed for the smallest signs of improvement, which came very slowly.

I remember one night when I woke to hear Katie crying. I got up and tried to comfort her, but nothing seemed to help. She was agitated and seemed to be in great pain. After an hour of unsuccessfully trying to comfort her, I knelt beside her bed and prayed earnestly. It was like magic—the magic of Jesus. She calmed instantly and went to sleep. I asked the Lord to make me free, unashamed, to pray openly in the hospital before the nurses and doctors. I refused to feel self-conscious before strangers when I was fighting for Katie's life.

After several months of fighting to regain her abilities in acute care at Children's Hospital, Katie transferred for rehab at the duPont Hospital for Children in Delaware.

I had resigned from my job to care for Katie at the Children's Hospitals while going home on weekends to be with my two boys in middle school. After fighting for her life, Katie struggled mightily to regain all her lost abilities. It was so challenging for all of us.

Some weeks were very hard. One of the lowest points I had emotionally came one Sunday night when I was overwhelmed and missing

Katie. I longed to hold her tight, to hear her sing and laugh. When I got up the next morning, I was weary already, and then Andy said he was too sick to go to school. Then Nate didn't want to get up and missed catching the bus. I broke down weeping and cried out to the Lord, "This is so hard. Please help me!" Later, as I was heading to the hospital, I remembered Isaiah 61:3, and I sang, "Lord, almighty God, comforter, Your Word is always what I need."

Again I was in a terrible pit, but this time the Lord was with me. My expectations changed dramatically, though I still had expectancy in the Lord to take care of us. My mother would say, "What are you going to do? How are you going to take care of her? What will you do when she's older?" And I would say, "I don't know. I'm just going to do what I can do today, and tomorrow I am going to do what I can do tomorrow. I'm just going to expect that the Lord will do something." He always has.

So, I began to live one day at a time. That's a really healthy place to be. I know you have to think about your future, but you can only do something today; you can't do something in the future. So you have to live one day at a time. Some people get frustrated with my living one day at a time. But it would be good for people who are always making plans to try to learn to live day by day.

I learned to wait on the Lord to see what He would do instead of me telling Him what He should do. I had questions and a few answers: *Who will house the boys for the week while I am with Katie?* My church family did. *Why was my innocent child hurt? Why are we suffering so? How will I get a new car? Why do I have to wrestle with things that are so difficult? Where was God when I needed Him?* Lots of questions.

In the hospital with Katie, I learned not to ask *why* questions, but *what* questions: *What are You doing, Lord? What do You want me to do? What do I need to do to get through this day? What way do You want me to respond?*

I remember sitting by Katie's bed in ICU and surrendering her to God and being able to say, "Thank You, God, for six beautiful years with Katie. Whatever You do with her, I give her to You because I am not in control. She's not mine; she is Yours. And I thank You for the time with her." That weekend when I went home to see my sons, they looked different. They looked all grown-up, independent, and I knew I was not in control of them either. They were mine to steward, to teach, to invest in, but they were not mine to control because I was not in control. So another surrender. I had to surrender all of my family.

In the hospital and rehab, people knew I was a follower of Christ because the other first-graders in Katie's class made giant posters that said "Jesus" on them, and they were all over our walls. They recognized us as those "Jesus freaks." Whenever my church friends came to visit, we were always playing Christian music, laying hands on Katie, and praying for her.

So I would try to help people, try to be Jesus for them by listening and comforting, but frankly, I wasn't very good at it because I was hurting so much myself. I fell far short of putting the Father on display, but in trying to help other people find answers, I found mine. One lady came into the room and asked me, "If your Jesus is so good and powerful, why did He let my child be born with spina bifida?"

I groped for an answer. "I don't know. He is God, and I am not. But if you knew Him, you would know that He is with you. If you walk through the fire, you will not be burned, and if you walk in deep water, you will not be drowned because God is there with you every step of the way." With His grace, mercy, and instruction, we got through that incredibly hard season.

Over the next eight years, I was a single mother with three children, and I was the full-time caretaker for Katie. I had no job for about a year, so I could help Katie recover. I learned to rely on the Lord and my church family, the body of Christ around me. They were His hands and feet. Friends raised funds to help support me. They replaced my destroyed car. They brought me food. Many times money was mysteriously deposited into my bank account by unknown benefactors. Other times cards of encouragement with cash came at the perfect time. My church was also very generous.

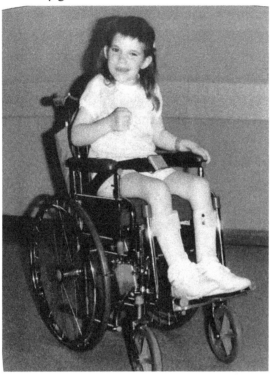

Katie struggled mightily to overcome her adversity. She was in the duPont Children's Hospital for almost five months of rehabilitation. Then Katie began a long, painfully slow journey, trying to regain as much of her mental and physical abilities as possible. Her right side was paralyzed, her speech was significantly impaired, and she suffered from epileptic seizures. She went back to her Christian school in the fall for her first-grade class. I had total faith in the Lord and in His amazing provision to take care of my family while I focused on caring for Katie.

Over the years that followed, Katie regained most of her cognitive abilities, except for her speech. Schoolwork was very challenging and took her much longer to accomplish. I was so proud of her and how hard she worked. She was able to stay at grade level through graduation in 1999. Since King's Christian Academy's high school was new, the classes were very small, and Katie was the valedictorian of the very first graduating class. I will never forget her speech. It was short, sweet, and to the point: "See ya!"

God, always faithful, had fulfilled His promise. There is no life so bruised and broken that God cannot mend it!

Behold, I make all things new. (Rev. 21:5 NKJV)

2

CHILDHOOD MEMORIES— MOLLY'S MEMORIES OF HER EARLY YEARS

I taught literature for many years, and literature often depicts a journey. We all begin at birth, and I'm going to share my journey with you.

I'll begin at the very beginning of my life in 1948 because I want to give you the whole picture of who I was and who I am now.

I was born in a rural farm community just south of Lake Erie, Pennsylvania. My dad, Roger Rose, was a farmer, and my extended family were all farmers, and we always had plenty. We had land, we had food, and we had good neighbors. I had a very safe and secure and happy childhood. We didn't think about whether we were rich or poor; we were all the same as our neighbors.

My older brother Ron has some great perspectives about our rich rural life: "When Molly was six years old, we moved about a mile up the road to open a small country general store across the road from our aunt and uncle and three cousins, who ran a small country food store— two shopping carts—surrounded by fields and farms. Barb, only eight years old, and Molly, just six, worked in the store and learned how to run a small business while we boys worked on local farms—mostly relatives. Our dad was one of ten children, so we had lots of uncles, aunts, and cousins living nearby. At one time, within an area of about five square miles, there were more than twenty-five Roses with the same address, R.D. #2, Waterford, Pennsylvania. The mailman just knew all the different Rose family members. Some of us went to one-room schools, and we all shared the same phone line. That close community, in itself, doesn't produce a person with Molly's talents and caring heart, but it helps. We had no idea how lucky we were to have so many caring relatives close by with whom to share birthdays and holidays, to play, and to help. We didn't realize until we were older that we were rich beyond measure. We thought this was how everyone lived. Molly was very bright. I'm sure you won't be surprised to hear that she was valedictorian of her high school senior class.

"Our sister Barb remembers Molly saying, 'Hey, we can do that,' or 'I can do that,' whatever the challenge, despite the lack of experience—and this was before the Internet. When Barb got married, nobody in our orbit had money. How do you pay for a wedding dress, ask the bridesmaids to buy gowns, and so on? Molly said, 'Hey, I can do that,' and she designed and made Barb's wedding dress, all the bridesmaids' dresses, and the flower girl's dress!

"Molly's education started a lifelong devotion to teaching and helping others, in addition to her practical skills of sewing, cooking, baking, inventing games and plays, and so on. Whether writing or producing plays, directing them, making the costumes, or learning to be a clown so she could entertain children, Molly tackled it all with enthusiasm and success—all the while making it a teaching moment for so many kids—and adults."

MOLLY'S EXPECTATIONS

I had the same expectations that the other girls in my family had. I would go to high school and get married and raise my children on a local farm. That's what my sister did, and she still lives there. But my brother Ron went to college, and I wanted to go too. I got a scholarship to a college in the city and went there.

I graduated with honors and got a graduate assistantship at Ohio State University. I graduated there and at twenty-two had a master's degree and no college debt. I was cooking! Everything was going according to my expectations—except now I had a career on top of my original expectations.

I came to Saint Mary's County, Maryland, to teach at Great Mills High School in 1971. In short order, I got married,had three wonderful children, a career that I loved, and we owned our own home. I thought the future was determined, and everything was great. It met all my expectations. And then, everything changed.

A man's heart plans his way, but the Lord directs his steps. (Prov. 16:9 NKJV)

3

MOLLY'S NEW LIFE— MOLLY'S MEMORIES OF HER EARLY YEARS

*I*was shocked and saddened when very unexpectedly, to me, my life fell apart in 1984. I'd always thought I had a good marriage. Everything seemed fine until that day when my husband, Mike, told me that he had fallen in love with another teacher from his school. He didn't love me anymore. He was leaving me for another woman.

That was the first major crisis in my life. Suddenly I was a single parent. My Katie was four, Nathan was nine, and Andy was eleven. They were all struggling just like I was. Life was much more difficult. I was in the pit financially, physically, emotionally. I was pretty desperate; I was ready to give up.

My neighborhood friends did anything they could think of that would bring me closer to the Lord, but I was pretty resistant. I had a neighbor, Jeanine, who lived right next door who would come across the lawn with a little tray, and there would be brownies on the plate with a bit of Scripture and a flower that she'd probably picked while she walked across my lawn. She was beautiful, a Southern belle of a lady.

"Jeanine, you know I don't really believe in the Scriptures. I don't know what's in the Bible. I don't know about that," I would say.

She would reply, "Oh, it doesn't matter. I thought it would just cheer you up."

And it was beautiful. Jeanine knew then what you and I know now, that the Word of God is quick and powerful. It goes out and does not return void. So God's Word did not come back empty. The Lord kept appearing and appearing until I could no longer resist Him. When you are ready to give up, that's when the Lord comes. He intervened when I finally agreed to go to her church.

Lanny Clark was the pastor of Patuxent River Assembly of God. He was a man full of love and great wisdom. His message that Sunday had a profound impact on my life.

Pastor Lanny remembered that moment vividly:

"Worship was in full swing when this nagging impression would not leave me. With great reluctance, but unwilling to be disobedient to the leading of the Holy Spirit, I stopped the worship and read the following declaration: 'Do not harden your hearts as in the rebellion, in the day of trial in the wilderness, where your fathers tested Me, tried Me, and saw My works forty years. Therefore, I was angry with that generation and said, "They always go astray in their heart, and they have not known My ways." So I swore in My wrath, "They shall not enter My rest"'" (Heb. 3:8–11 NKJV).

Pastor Clark recalls that service:

"I did not know it, but at that very moment, Molly was visiting us for the first time. That word penetrated her troubled soul as she heard a word from the Lord just for her. It was the beginning of her introduction to the Lord Jesus and her maturation process within our church."

"Molly had been invited to our worship service by a compassionate neighbor who understood the distress Molly was experiencing: Molly's first husband had recently abandoned her and their three children. She was hurting and looking for some relief and comfort. She found Jesus and His representatives within our church caring, supportive, and understanding. The congregation embraced Molly and her children, and together they began the long road to recovery."

MOLLY'S TESTIMONY

I used to think I knew everything. Then in 1984, the Lord rescued me from the pit of divorce and showed me and my three children the love of God. After I committed my life to follow Jesus, I learned that I knew nothing of value. All that I thought was wise was revealed as foolishness; true wisdom waited for me to apprehend it.

My four-year-old Katie moved forward spiritually more quickly than the boys and I did. She was not burdened by the "sin that so easily ensnares us" (Heb. 12:1 NKJV) and was unabashedly excited and vocal about Jesus. You might think a spiritual conversion could not be dramatic in a young and innocent girl. She had no apparent addictions to erase, no besetting sins to deny, and no history of evil intentions and unkind acts to obliterate. Nevertheless, the transformation in Katie was noticeable. Another mother in her preschool asked me, "What did you do for Katie? She's so much happier lately," and a neighbor remarked, "Katie seems to be dealing with her loss better these days." For Katie, her new relationship with Jesus meant peace in her broken heart, a peace so real that others could see it. We rejoiced that God's love was alive inside her. His constant assurance shone right through in the daily behavior of a preschooler who leaned on Him.

Katie modeled for me what the Lord meant when He said, "I tell you the truth; anyone who doesn't receive the Kingdom of God like a little child will never enter it" (Mark 10:15 NLT).

We began to pursue the Lord. I had piles of denominational misconceptions I had picked up in childhood. These were covered by more layers of atheistic denials I would have to analyze and eradicate in my quest for truth. Katie had none of that and came to the Lord with an open mind and a clean heart. She accepted the truth simply, without question, without the need to find a niche where each new precept could fit without discomfort. Katie embraced God as her Father, gladly returned the friendship Jesus offered, and welcomed the comforting presence of His Holy Spirit. She expected everything she was taught to be unequivocally true, no questions asked. It would be years before I would arrive at anything near her confidence in God.

Once introduced to Him, Katie began immediately to communicate with God as she would with any new acquaintance. It was not uncommon for her, when caught in a spasm of frustration or a selfish bit of anger (she was, after all, a child!), to march off to her room to find the Lord. Minutes later, she'd come marching back with a lighter step, gleefully announcing, "I talked to Him!"

Once, I got up the nerve to plumb for what went on in these conversations, hoping I could learn her technique of on-the-spot attitude reversal.

I asked, "Katie, what does the Lord say to you when you talk to Him?"

"Oh, just stuff."

"What kind of stuff?"

"Lots of stuff."

I could see she was not sure how to categorize His words to her, so I made a guess, "Does He tell you what He wants you to do?"

She thought about this for a moment before giving me another vague answer. "No...not really...I don't think so."

"Does He say things that make you feel better?"

"Yes!"

"What does He say?"

"I don't know...just stuff...like, He pats me on my shoulder and says, 'It's okay, Katie.'"

You may attribute this, as I did, to the active imagination of a hurting child. Still, that explanation is wholly inadequate to explain a real, unprecedented life change in both behavior and outlook of a human of any age. Katie was having intimate conversations with the King of the universe. When we connect with God, change is inevitable—and delightful!

For the next couple of years, Katie and I went together on a journey of spiritual growth. There were, of course, areas where I had the advantage. I could read the Bible and take discipleship courses. I learned to write in a journal, to memorize scripture, to use a concordance, to take sermon notes, and to be accountable to fellow believers.

He lifted me out of the muck and mire. He put my feet on the rock and put a song in my heart. Psalm 140:12–13 became one of my favorite memory verses. I was exceedingly grateful to Him. That's when I surrendered, and that's why I waved my white flag during worship because this journey was all about surrender. When I surrendered to the Lord the very first time, I gave Him my whole life.

I put aside my expectations and my plans and my designs for the future and began to live in expectancy. I knew that the Lord was going to do something, even though I didn't know what it was. I began to want to follow His plan, whether I could see it or not, or whether it was what I thought I wanted or not. After the Lord entered my life, I felt like everything would be different. I believed that now I would go back to having some success in living because I was living surrendered to Him. I would trust Him that He would take care of my children and me. That was an excellent place to be.

My soul, wait silently for God alone, for my expectation is from Him. (Ps. 62:5 NKJV)

4

SOUL MATE FOREVER

Then, in the summer of 1993, the Lord sent a real rescuer to help me, Tim Frink. We had known each other for many years in the church. I always had great respect for him. We were in a small group together and occasionally talked about the challenges of being single parents. One night that summer, he called me to get counsel about challenges he was having with his girls. Katie listened to our conversation and talked to me about it afterward.

"Mom, we could adopt Tim and the girls."

"What!" I replied with a laugh, a bit startled. "Tim doesn't need a mother. He already has one."

Katie sheepishly grinned. "I meant a wife."

"Who's going to marry him—you or me?"

Giggling, Katie pointed at me.

"But I thought you didn't want me ever to get married again."

Katie gave a little grin and a big shrug.

"You don't think it would be so bad if it were Tim, right?"

Smiling broadly, Katie nodded her head and said, "Yeah."

That wonderful summer, Tim and I would fall in love, and he would become my beloved husband in 1994. Do you remember that Scripture in Ephesians where it says he can do above and beyond all that we can think and ask? God provided a husband who was far above all I could ever think of or ask for.

Tim became the head of our household, an advocate, a protector, a provider, and a loving father for Katie. He was indeed my Prince Charming.

I once told him, "The only person I trust more than me is you."

Tim laughed and responded, "Well, I trust you a lot more than I trust me because I agree with the prophet Jeremiah who says I have a wicked, deceitful heart!"

I felt secure, knowing I could trust him not to violate the values we shared and the principles that guided our lives. I felt blessed to have a husband whom so many people counted on at church and in various community ministries like HOPE and CareNet. Tim was a faithful man of integrity and character. I never had to worry about him ever being unfaithful to me.

I so appreciated Tim's resourcefulness and excellent ability to find solutions. I felt safe knowing that if I faced a serious problem, he would always try to help any way he could. I remember the time I got in a minor car accident. He was at work when I called him about the accident.

"Hi, Tim. I'm afraid that I've had a small car accident."

He immediately interrupted me. "Are you okay? Is Katie okay?" he asked, alarmed.

I assured him, "I think Katie bumped her head on her window when the car hit us, but we're both fine."

"Oh no. 'When the car hit you.' What happened?"

"Well, I was backing down the driveway, and I thought I'd looked both ways. But somehow, I backed right in front of a car coming down our street. Thank God she wasn't going fast. The driver said she saw me backing up and slowed down. She thought for sure I had seen her and would stop since I was going slow. But I didn't stop, so she hit me."

He laughed. "You mean, your accident was like one of those slow-motion bumper-car wrecks when two old ladies play chicken! I guess you deserved to get hit."

"Watch it, buddy," I retorted. "I may be older than you, but I'm not an old woman!"

"Molly, I'm so sorry. I didn't mean to call you an old lady. Please forgive me. It's okay. You are far more important to me than the car. I'll take care of it. I thank the Lord you and Katie are fine."

Even though I was quite upset, he wasn't upset with me at all. I felt protected and secure, grateful for the times he covered my errors and faults and gave me grace.

With Tim came two young stepdaughters, Katie and Christi. So now we had Andy and Nate in college and three girls in middle school: Christi, a sixth-grader; Katie Frink, a seventh-grader; and Katie Buonviri, in the eighth grade. We started calling my daughter "Katie B." to lessen confusion in the home. If you've ever had middle school girls, you know how challenging that can be. Due to Tim's recent divorce, even the two who were full sisters were really struggling.

Blending two families is challenging under the best circumstances, but it is especially hard when the kids are hurting. I remember strong disagreements over many things, some serious, some quite minor. One time Christi spent the weekend with us. Saturday morning, both girls came into the kitchen dressed in skimpy shirts and form-fitting tights. Tim and I explained to them we wanted them to dress more modestly when they were with us. They were not happy campers! Two sets of values and rules were tough on everyone. On many occasions, feeling like the wicked stepmother, I cried out to the Lord for more love and wisdom.

But that all changed over the years as I steadfastly loved them no matter what they said or did. I don't use the word *stepdaughter* anymore because they are truly my daughters, whom I love dearly. We faced challenges one day at a time, which is all that you can do in middle school or life. By God's grace, we became a real family.

TIM'S JOURNAL ENTRY, MAY 1993

I am so thankful I have been able to go camping in the Shenandoah Valley. I needed time away from all of my challenges at home with the girls. I need time to think about my life and what the Lord wants for my family and me. Rita has been gone for over six months, and she has made it clear she is never coming back. She wants a divorce; the sooner, the better, especially now that she is with a new man.

Molly has been a very special godsend to me. She's in the small group I am now attending, led by Peter and Barbara Prentice. She's been a good friend to me ever since Rita left as I struggle with raw emotions of hurt, anger, and confusion. I have feelings I've never experienced before—deep, painful feelings of rejection and remorse, and gut-wrenching feelings of regret, sorrow, grief, despair, and more tears than I've cried in my lifetime. Sometimes I have terrible feelings of cold, hard anger toward Rita. I have many questions. How can this destruction of my family be happening to my precious girls and me?

Molly is one of the few people who understands what I am going through. She went through the same experience nine years ago when her husband rejected her and abandoned her family. I've known Molly for years, ever since Katie's accident. I've always admired her simple, child-like faith, putting God to the test, proving His Word, and watching His miraculous provision.

When you lose somebody to divorce after many years of conflict, you gain perspective about highly esteemed character qualities. Given the opportunity to start over again, you can be wiser and more careful in your relationships.

There are many character qualities that I highly esteem in Molly or any woman I might marry. First and foremost, Molly is a woman who loves the Lord, her God, with all of her heart, soul, mind, and strength. Through eight years of struggle after the divorce and Katie's accident, she's developed a deep faith and a mature relationship with Jesus. Her great suffering and sorrow have produced a vibrant, childlike faith that has always impressed me. There are very few people who understand the Father, His love, and His ways the way she does.

Molly is a woman of prayer. She's fought in the heavens for the life and the recovery of precious Katie. She has an intimate relationship with Jesus, her Savior. She daily communes with Him, seeking His wisdom, direction, and provision.

Molly is a woman of love. Her love of children is evident for everyone to see. She has laid her life down not only for her own family but for many other children as well. The loving way she cares for children in our church shows the depth of her love for others. True love is dying to self for the benefit of another.

Molly is truly a servant who loves to help people. I remember a clown skit she performed where many people asked her to help them. Time after time, Molly replied, "Okay, I can do that," until it finally dawned on her that she needed two more Mollys to do everything she'd promised. I'm sure Molly did that skit because it revealed an everyday struggle in her life. I love people who have the heart of a servant. They are the heart and soul of Christian ministry. Without them, very little would be accomplished in the kingdom of God. Her humble, selfless service is just what Jesus commanded us to do: "The greatest among you must be a servant."

Molly is a woman with a great sense of humor. She's clever and fun to be around. Molly even enjoys my unusual sense of humor, which often causes my girls to say, "Oh, Dad, you are so corny!" She loves to take her clown troupe to the nursing home, do skits, tell funny stories, and help the residents laugh.

Molly is a very intelligent, thoughtful woman. Recently, I have been calling her with family problems, and we talked at great length about the deep things of God and the ways He works in our lives. She's always learning about the Lord both for her benefit and to help others. I love talking to close friends about the Lord's profound truths.

These are just a few essential character qualities that I treasure in Molly and in any woman that I might marry. I look to God for His plans for me. I am hoping to marry again someday, a woman who will be my best friend, to grow old together and serve the Lord until we die. King Solomon expresses my feelings best:

> **Charm is deceitful, and beauty is passing, but a woman who fears the Lord, she shall be praised. (Prov. 31:30 NKJV)**

5

BRIANNA JONES—OUR AMAZING LITTLE BUTTERFLY

*M*y daughter, Christianna Frink, met Christopher Jones in the Army's military-police training school in the early summer of 2008. They had both previously been in the military before joining the Army. Chris was a Marine but then transferred to the Army and served a tour in Iraq. Christi served two deployments as a medical technician in the Air Force. She had helped take care of wounded soldiers transported from Iraq to Germany and the Hurricane Katrina evacuation effort.

Their first daughter, Brianna Jones, was born on March 27, 2009, in El Paso, Texas, where they were stationed. Her little sister, Alexis Jones, was born fourteen months later, in May 2010. Shortly afterward, the Army transferred them to Fort Campbell, Kentucky. Christi and Chris got orders to go back to Iraq in February 2011. We all agreed to have their children stay with Christi's mother's family, and with us, for the nine months they would be gone.

At first, I couldn't believe they wanted to leave their precious little girls with us and go off to war together rather than having one parent go away while the other parent took care of the children. But they thought it would be less stressful for their marriage and their children to serve their tours at the same time and have us grandparents take care of the girls. It turned out to be one of the greatest years of our lives, a year we will never forget.

Parenting young grandchildren can be a very challenging experience, as some of you may already know. Their energy, their emotions, their challenges can really stretch grandparents to the limit. But reliving our children's early years and experiencing the joys and the delights that we could have with these precious little girls was beyond imagination.

A few entries from my journal in that first year when they lived with us show that Brianna Jones was indeed an extraordinary little girl.

Brianna, when you first came to Maryland, you were just twenty-three months old, and your sister was nine months old. I used to come home early from work and watch you for two hours till your grandmother picked you up. I would hold you and read stories and take you up to the school to play. You amazed me with your strength and agility as you climbed the monkey bars like a big kid. You could even go across the monkey bars rung by rung with a little help from Grandpa.

You loved the story of the big bad wolf and the two little kids. Whenever we played big bad wolf in our playground fort, you'd say, "Don't be afraid, big bad wolf; don't be afraid!" when you were the one half-terrified.

You were only two years old, but you loved to fly kites. I remember when we went to Leonardtown after Hurricane Irene, and the wind was blowing so strong. You wanted to fly my kite because you were a big girl. You took that string and ran and ran across that huge, long field and watched in utter delight as the kite soared behind you while I chased after you calling, "Brianna, come back." You never looked back once; you were so captivated by that kite.

You were so good with words and expressing yourself at such a young age. You always amazed us with your delightful expressions. I'll never forget the time we were driving to the top of the bridge to Solomons Island,

and you first looked and beheld the beautiful view of the Patuxent River and the Chesapeake Bay. From the backseat, we heard your joyful exclamation as you threw your arms out and proclaimed, "It's amazing!" I remember one time we were playing cards, and you held out a handful of cards, and you said, "Pick a card, any card," as though you were a professional card shark in Las Vegas.

You were wise beyond your years and so mature. I remember one day when you were disappointed that we couldn't go swimming at the pool, even though you told me, "But I love swimming." Then, when you couldn't play on the playground due to the sweltering heat, you said, "But I love playgrounds." Finally, we decided to drop Grandma Molly off at Walmart, and then I would take you to Oma's home. We didn't have time for you to go shopping, and you said, "But I love shopping." Instead of throwing a temper tantrum like a typical two-year-old who is utterly frustrated, you sat quietly in the backseat. Then, in a little voice, I heard you say, "I'm so mad I feel like hitting the car!" I felt so guilty that I got you girls ice cream on the way to Oma's house.

You loved to ride on my shoulders and shout out with glee with one of your funny sayings, "Look how high my are." You loved to play games and have fun and dance like a princess. I remember at your Aunt Katie's wedding that you danced nonstop for almost two hours, even joining the bride and groom for their special dance. You were a bright ray of sunshine, giving us joy and delight. Whenever I see a golden butterfly, I think of you because you loved our flower garden and the multitude of dancing butterflies flitting from flower to flower. It has truly been a magical summer.

INCREDIBLE HEARTBREAK

When Christi and Chris returned from Iraq in December 2011, we were thankful for their safe return. Their family was reunited for seven months and lived in Clarksville, Tennessee, at Fort Campbell. On July 10, 2012, while I was in Houston, Texas, at a business conference, I received the horrible news that Brianna, my precious granddaughter, had been strangled to death by a blind cord in the upstairs den.

Christi and Chris had awakened to another day of military service and caring for Brianna, three, and Alexis, two. Brianna put on her bride costume and coaxed Daddy into marrying her with Mommy officiating, one of her favorite pretend games. Then Daddy went off to the base, and Mommy had the day off to spend with the girls. Later that day, Christi was in the kitchen with Alexis doing some mother-daughter baking. Brianna was just at the top of the stairs in the family den, watching her favorite TV show. When Christi hadn't heard any jumping or singing for a while, she headed up the stairs to investigate why Brianna was so quiet.

You cannot imagine the shock and horror my daughter felt when she went upstairs to check on Brianna and discovered her limp body hanging there, strangled to death by a blind cord. Christi, having CPR training, grabbed poor Brianna and began lifesaving procedures, all the time knowing it was too late. She then called 911 and Chris, and he raced home just in time to see the ambulance take his little bride away forevermore.

I was in Dallas for a conference and walking through the airport when I got the call from Christi's mom telling me the terrible news. I was devastated beyond words and broke down sobbing, "No, no, no, no God, no! This can't be real. She can't be dead. Brianna, my precious Brianna, my poor baby, is gone. Why, why, why, why?"

Later that night, after very painful, tearful calls with Christi and Molly, I wrote the following in my journal:

My heart is broken; my head hurts from so many tears I can hardly think. My heart breaks for poor Christi, poor Chris. I hurt so bad for them, for their loss, for their pain. I can't imagine the hell they are experiencing right now. If my soul is crushed beyond words, how broken and desperate they must be. Overwhelming grief like the blackest night takes my breath away. Oh, God, why have You taken my precious grandbaby away?

Nine years later, we all have emotional scars from this horrible experience, but we have survived. Over the years, the pain deep in our souls has diminished. But we never forget; Brianna is forever in our souls. You see, Molly and I not only lost our granddaughter, but we felt like we'd lost our own precious little child. The impact upon our kids was devastating beyond words; you never fully recover from the sudden death of a child. Christopher retired on disability from the army due to severe injuries suffered in Iraq to both knees. Chris and Christi both developed severe PTSD from traumatic war experiences and the loss of dear Brianna. They lost their army careers and are now retired on disability. They were extremely fortunate that their love and commitment to each other was so strong that they didn't lose their marriage, as often happens to families that have lost young children.

> *What we have once enjoyed and deeply loved we can never lose,*
> *for all that we love deeply becomes a part of us.*
>
> —*Helen Keller*

MOLLY'S UNIQUE PERSPECTIVE

Tim and I were both out of town in different places. I was visiting my mother, and Tim was away at a conference. When I got home, there was a distraught message on the answering machine from our daughter Christi saying, "Daddy, call me back as soon as you can. Brianna is gone." I hoped that our beautiful three-year-old granddaughter had wandered off and that they had found her by now. But that was not the truth; the truth was that she was dead! She had been accidentally strangled in the Venetian blind cords in her home.

It was an immense heartbreak and another opportunity to ask, "Lord, where were You?" We had been very close to Brianna because she and her younger sister, Alexis, who was a baby, had stayed here in St. Mary's County with us. They lived with the other grandparents and stayed with us for a couple of nights each week. Many of our friends knew Brianna because we often took her to church. She was a precious, precious child. And we dearly loved her. I had learned from my experience with Katie to press into the Lord and surrender to Him. I had to do that again.

Peace. I had to learn to live in God's peace and to listen to Him. He showed me a picture of Brianna's life. She was like a little butterfly. She was beautiful and colorful. She was so active and full of joy; she was a delightful child. She came into our lives like a butterfly, and for a very short time she brought us great joy. I realized that was all there was for her life. All of our days are ordained for us in His book before any one of them comes to be. Those were all her days. And though her life was very short, it was complete. I realize now there were no tragedies to come, no depression, no pain, to mark Brianna's life. She was just a little complete bundle of joy. I still know her that way, and I'm going to see her in heaven. So we got through another crisis by surrendering everything to the Lord and listening to what He had to say.

You will keep him in perfect peace, whose mind is stayed on You Because he trusts in You. (Isa. 26:3 NKJV)

6

SWALLOW FALLS—JUNE 2018

*M*olly retired from The King's Christian Academy several years ago, where she'd taught English and theater for over twenty years. She started volunteering at the school one day a week with Katie, helping out in the library. She loved the ministry of CareNet Pregnancy Center, which helps people facing an unplanned pregnancy, so she and Katie helped sort all of the donations of baby clothes.

In her retirement, Molly was able to spend more time with her beloved grandsons in Philadelphia. She was also deeply committed to three young church families: the Jamersons, McOmbers, and Zeilers. Their fourteen children loved her dearly. She was their Grandma Molly. After she retired, Molly focused more time and attention on taking care of Katie, whose mind and body had been in decline over the last twenty years.

Molly turned seventy years old in April and was overwhelmed by a surprise celebration I organized at our son Nate's home in Philadelphia. She was so delighted, visiting with her dearly beloved extended family, playing cards late into the night, and catching up on family news.

In June, we went camping at our favorite campground, Swallow Falls State Park, with our dear friends, the Jamersons and their seven kids, and the Friess family. We had often camped with Christi and Katie Frink in this beautiful state park in western Maryland. It is at the confluence of two small rivers and had campsites nestled under magnificent hemlock trees. Paths alongside the rivers were full of giant old-growth hemlocks, rhododendrons, mountain laurel, and giant cinnamon ferns. It is truly a magical place with quiet pools of water in mountain cathedrals with altars of mossy boulders and windows made of sky. We loved walking the paths along the rivers, resting by serene pools, and worshiping the Creator of such deep, quiet woods.

Muddy Creek, the smaller of the two rivers, has a majestic torrent of water hurtling over forty-foot-high cliffs, creating a beautiful waterfall. The Youghiogheny River has a series of rapids spilling down rocky chutes, over ledges, and into many deep pools. Adults and children enjoy sliding down the slimy rocks on the natural waterslides. There is also a huge swimming hole where, in the past, we had enjoyed leaping off the boulders and swimming behind the small waterfalls.

We had three campsites side by side, and everybody assembled at ours since we had all the supplies and the big tarp over the eating area. We thanked the Lord for the tarp because it rained on and off for all four days. The children gravitated to Molly: visiting, eating, talking, taking turns sitting on her lap, doing various projects, and playing games with her.

The second night as we lay down to sleep, Molly remarked, "I am so tired. I can't believe how busy my day has been."

"If I did as many things as you did with those kids, I'd be exhausted too," I agreed, "and I'm not nearly as old as you are!"

"I know," she replied, "but I enjoy being with these children so much. They are great fun. Watching their delight when we do things together brings such joy to my soul."

"Maybe tomorrow you could rest a little bit more and just sit by the campfire and talk with them," I suggested. "You don't have to help with all the cooking, cleanup, and entertaining the children. Your spirit is willing, but your flesh is weaker than it used to be."

Each night, we gathered everyone around the campfire with their marshmallow sticks for making s'mores. Molly helped the younger children roast their marshmallows to a perfect puff of brown without getting too close to the fire. When we gathered around the fire in camping chairs, the young children would clamor, "Grandma, Grandma. I want to sit on your lap. Please, Grandma!" Every child knew they were unique and deeply treasured by their beloved Grandma Molly.

With all the rain in the previous month, the river ran high and fast with white-water rapids covering rocks and pools. One day while we watched kayakers race down the tumultuous rapids, Molly had baby Sophia on her lap and watched the children play in shallow pools along the river's edge. She had this small smile on her face, perfectly content, delighting in God, His precious children, and His glorious creation. It is a perfect picture I will forever treasure.

As we were getting ready to leave Sunday morning, we decided to have a mini-church service on the small stage at the campground amphitheater. After prayer and worship, Molly decided it was time for a little drama. Of course, when Molly got close to a stage, she became a director again. She loved watching a story come alive in children's hearts and minds, enjoyed interacting with them and watching them grow into their parts. One of her greatest joys was seeing a scared or shy student bring a character to life on the stage.

With this small stage crying out for a show, Molly immediately recruited Ethan, age seven, to join her for a skit.

"Ethan, look at all of these people," said Molly.

"Yeah, who made them?"

"God made them," Molly replied. "God made all of these beautiful people."

"But, Grandma, who made all the ugly ones?"

Ethan then collapsed, howling with laughter and delight, tickled with his first role. Molly beamed with joy.

STRANGE SYMPTOMS OVER THE SUMMER

Molly had always been full of energy, able to take long walks with me through the beautiful woods every day. This vacation was different. She tired quickly, was less talkative and quieter, even around the children at the campfires.

She never complained, but one day told me, "I guess once you turn seventy, you just start wearing out more easily."

We didn't give it much thought at the time, chalking it up to getting older and going slower. Molly's stomach started swelling over the summer. We thought it was maybe an allergy to gluten or celiac disease or something else, but Molly did not want to see her doctor. She had always been in such good health throughout her life; she would only go when she was desperately ill or injured. Molly came from a long line of long-lived farm families with grandmothers living into their late nineties. She always tried to eat right, except brownies and ice cream, and was still active and busy helping with the church, school, friends, or family. Molly enjoyed the challenge of walking ten thousand steps every day. She had a pedometer, which she checked religiously throughout the day to make sure she was on track.

Then, in July, Molly started having occasional sharp pains in her abdomen that alarmed us both. We thought she had digestive issues. But they kept coming back, and she finally made an appointment to see our family doctor after our annual Erie vacation in August, one of her favorite times of the year. Molly's brother Ron describes her close-knit family and their annual reunion:

"We carry our closeness to the present day as we attend the Rose family reunion every year outside of Erie, Pennsylvania, with about one hundred relatives. Molly, Tim, and Katie are always there. August 2018 was our sixty-fourth consecutive reunion. The five of us siblings, our spouses, and some of our families gather in a large rented ski chalet for a full week before the reunion on Sunday. And we don't argue—we don't talk about religion, and we don't talk about politics—we reminisce, we share meals, we laugh, and we coexist under one roof because we truly enjoy each other's company. And we play games—a few of us sometimes stay up until three in the morning playing cards or Trivial Pursuit. Molly was a trooper, always one of the last ones to go to bed, except this year. Now she was tired all the time and went to bed much earlier."

We should have known something was seriously wrong. However, Molly wasn't worried at all. She was sure it was something minor. Molly didn't fear the worst but was at peace. She always hoped for the best.

The peace of God, which transcends all understanding, will guard your hearts and minds through Christ Jesus. **(Phil. 4:7 NIV)**

Molly Rose, 13 years old.

Molly Rose, 22 years old in the jacket she made.

Molly, Andy, Nate, Katie one year after the accident in 1987.

January 15, 1994. A wonderful new life for Tim and Molly Frink.

Nate and Maria Buonviri wedding in 2003.

Jamerson family: Brian, Anita, Samantha,
Shauna, Alex, Nathan, Ethan, Sara, Sophia.

Jones family: Chris & Christi, Brianna, and Alexis.

Tim & Molly full of joy.

Christmas 2009 with Andy & Ariadna Bounviri,
Nate & Maria, Carlo, Paolo, and Matteo Buonviri.

The annual Rose family pyramid:
Barb Galkowski, Molly, David, Ron, and Mark Rose.

7

WHAT IS WRONG
WITH MOLLY?

TUESDAY, AUGUST 14, 2018

*M*olly had her sonogram done on Monday. The physician's assistant called her late Tuesday afternoon to say the sonogram showed a buildup of fluid in the abdomen and that she should get a CT scan as soon as possible. So she immediately went to the ER at St. Mary's Hospital for the scan. I stayed home with Katie. It was a little disquieting, but neither of us was worried.

Molly called me later with the bad news. "Tim, the CT scan confirmed that I have fluid in my abdomen. It needs to be drained and tested. I can't come home. They want to admit me and run more tests tomorrow."

I stood in shocked silence. Questions started racing in my mind, dark clouds scuttling before an impending storm.

"Did they say what could be causing the fluid buildup? How serious is it?" I anxiously asked.

"I don't know. The doctor told me not to worry."

"Tim, God is in control, and I trust Him."

We discussed plans for Katie's care so that I could spend the next day with Molly. We then prayed together and encouraged ourselves with His promises: *"You will keep him in perfect peace whose mind is stayed on You because he trusts in You"* (Isa. 26:3).

When I visited Molly the next day, she was comfortable in the nicely decorated hospital room. We chatted for a while, and then I read our newest book to her, one of our favorite pastimes. We both loved to read and always had multiple books going at the same time. We spent the day talking, reading, and visiting with friends who dropped by.

After a couple of days of tests, I was anxious to get her out of the hospital and home as soon as possible. I knew it must be serious when Molly told me, "Tim, please stop being so concerned about taking me home. I am not ready to go just yet; I just need some time to rest. They are taking good care of me."

Friends and family continued calling and visiting to get updates and offered their love to their beloved Molly. The days passed in a blur of juggling care for Katie, hospital visits, doctor exams, tests, and more tests. Every doctor assured her they didn't think it was dangerous since the tests were negative. An OB-GYN said, "You don't need to be concerned. The CT scan is clear and shows no sign of tumors on the uterus or the ovaries. It's probably nothing serious."

Molly was not so optimistic. "Why am I so tired, why is my belly full of fluid, and why do I have this painful lump in my belly?"

We waited all day Friday for the specialist to come, the hours passing slowly, to discuss the results of her MRI. It was a battle, but we refused to fear the worst and were hoping for the best. We talked quietly about how this crisis was affecting our five kids and six grandchildren. They were all very concerned, and all were offering prayers for her health and recovery.

Finally, at 6:00 p.m., a new specialist came to see Molly, a middle-aged doctor, one of the many from India in our community. "Hello, Mrs. Frink. I am Dr. Shah, an oncologist. I have been reviewing your scans and test results." We sat in shocked silence. *No, no, no, this can't be happening,* I cried out deep within my soul. A cancer doctor was the last specialist we expected.

Dr. Shah explained the tests. "There are three markers we examine to see if there are any cancer cells from the colon, the ovaries, or other major organs. We don't see any large tumors on any of your organs, just some small irregularities on your pancreas and a thickening of the sheath tissue around the intestines called the omentum. Since there's no sign of major organ failure, which could cause the fluid buildup, our next step is to eliminate all other possibilities. I should have the results later next week. We will meet next Friday to discuss the test results. In the meantime, go home and rest."

We were relieved Molly didn't have any evident signs that it was cancer, but on our drive home, we discussed the unexpected possibility.

Molly shook her head, "I can't believe they think I might have cancer. None of the doctors seemed overly concerned. I'm sure it's not that serious. We just need to trust the Lord with all our heart and lean not on our own understanding; in all our ways, we must acknowledge Him. He will direct our paths."

I appreciated Molly's faith but was deeply troubled. Something was seriously wrong with my beloved wife, my dearest friend. I desperately hoped it was not cancer. We needed all the prayer cover we could get to battle for Molly's health and life. After getting home, I sent out word to our family and many friends in our church and other churches to join us in prayer for Molly.

ANOTHER DARK DAY WITH VERY BAD NEWS
Friday, August 24, 2018

We waited in a nondescript examination room at Dr. Shah's oncology center. The room had sterile off-white walls and various posters about the human body. We weren't anxious but hopeful that our prayers and our loved ones' prayers would bring good news.

When Dr. Shah finally came in, she quietly greeted us and shuffled her papers, then looked into Molly's eyes and said with tender compassion, "I am very sorry, Mrs. Frink, but the tests on the fluid in your abdomen indicate you have stage 4 cancer. The peritoneal fluid is full of cancer cells, and all three cancer marker tests show signs of cancer, which has spread to other vital organs. There is no cure for cancer once it has spread to multiple organs."

I sat in shocked silence, unable to breathe. It seemed the air had been sucked from the room. Molly was quiet and unemotional. She did not cry as she calmly stared into the face of death. But I was devastated by the diagnosis of terminal cancer. The doctor's words were massive boulders in my heart and dragged me under churning waves of emotion. They engulfed me and threatened to suffocate me. I could barely breathe, let alone think, much less ask the right questions. How could this happen? Molly wasn't in severe pain; she was still active and full of life. We knew we could fight against stage 1, 2, or 3 cancer, but since the cancer had spread so much, we didn't know how Molly could survive. We spent an hour talking to the doctor about Molly's cancer and various treatment options.

"Further tests," continued Dr. Shah, "will determine the type of cancer, where it came from, and where it is located. Surgery and chemotherapy may help slow the disease and drive it into remission, but it will return. We won't know how long you might live until we determine the full extent of the disease."

The doctor ordered a PET scan and other tests to refine the prognosis. Then Molly would have exploratory surgery to determine the extent of the disease and determine the treatment plan.

We refused to allow fear to consume us. We would not be dismayed with the deadly prognosis. We knew the Lord would give us strength and help us triumph in the storm that would be crashing around us in the days ahead. We agreed to cling to the Lord's right hand, and His promises of healing found throughout the Bible. We both had walked with the Lord for many decades and seen Him heal us and others many times over the years. We knew He was still in the healing business. We knew Jesus loved Molly and would not leave her nor forsake her.

When we got home, we sat on the deck and discussed what to do next. Many scriptures we had memorized long ago came to mind, encouraged us, and gave us hope.

> *Fear not, for I am with you; do not be dismayed, for I am your God. I will strengthen you and help you; I will uphold you with my righteous right hand. (Isa. 40:31 NKJV)*

8

SHOCKING NEWS—"THAT WOULD BE A MIRACLE!"

Johns Hopkins University Hospital
FRIDAY, SEPTEMBER 14, 2018

"*I*am very sorry, but the results of the exploratory surgery show that cancer has spread everywhere throughout Molly's abdomen. It's in the omentum, the ovaries, with spots on the liver, pancreas, and all over the peritoneum. We cannot operate to remove her cancer. There is no cure for this cancer. The best we can offer is six months of very potent chemotherapy and then reevaluate."

Stunned, I asked Dr. Greer, her surgeon, if there was any way the chemotherapy could destroy all the cancer and save her life. He shook his head and sadly replied, "That would be a miracle!" I thanked the doctor and turned away, crestfallen and brokenhearted.

Time stopped moving. I looked around the waiting room and stared at the walls in disbelief. Tears welled up as I contemplated the terrible future that awaited Molly and me. We had all been praying for the past four weeks for miraculous healing, not this devastating news. I could not believe that the brightest light in my life—my precious, amazingly loving wife of almost twenty-five years—could soon have her life snuffed out like a candle and plunge my life into darkness.

The last six years since Brianna's death had passed in a blur, the clouds of our grief blown away and replaced by the warm sun. Our lives were full of activities at church, school, and with our family and friends. Ever since Molly's retirement several years ago, we had been looking forward to spending more time with each other, traveling, and visiting our families in Philadelphia, Colorado, and Michigan. Now all of our dreams lay shattered around us like a beautiful vase dropped on the floor.

Surgery to remove the cancer was no longer an option, and even chemotherapy could not cure Molly; at best, it would give her only a few extra months to live. Our Lord was truly our only hope. I desperately cried out, "I surrender Molly to You, dear Jesus, and put my trust in You alone. I believe that You can perform a miracle and save Molly from certain death. All we have to cling to is You. You are our shepherd and our comfort in our affliction, for Your Word has given us life."

Most people wonder how they would respond to a dire prognosis that they have only a very short time to live. In what ways would you change your life? Would you quit your job and set out to accomplish everything on your bucket list? Would you try to get away and visit some exotic places? Would you focus on yourself and spend all of your time and energy trying to cling to life, desiring to experience every moment to the fullest because it truly could be your last? Would you be angry and lash out at God?

Or would you keep on living a joy-filled life and loving those people who are the most precious to you? Would you be willing to embrace your family and your dear friends and walk down a path toward probable death arm in arm, cheek to cheek?

Molly, who had suffered so many tragedies over the years, chose to live her life full of love and full of faith. She decided to live her days, as she always had, devoted to those she cherished. Molly's great love, trust, and strength of character came from her relationship with her Lord, her wonderful family, and her many dear friends.

JOHNS HOPKINS UNIVERSITY HOSPITAL RECOVERY ROOM, FROM TIM'S JOURNAL

After meeting with Dr. Greer, I am waiting for Molly to awaken while I try to process her terminal diagnosis. My hardest struggle is staying focused on the present, not racing ahead, imagining the worst, and trying to plan for a future without Molly. I have a myriad of questions for my Lord:

How will I survive the loss of my best friend, the lover of my soul?

How will I live without the greatest gift God has ever given me?

What will we do with Katie, with all of her severe disabilities?

How will Katie survive the loss of her mother? Ever since the car accident thirty-two years ago, Molly has been her lifelong helper, her encourager, her comforter, her closest friend. I can't take care of her; I will have to place her in a nursing home. You know how hard that will be for her. This life and this home are all she has ever known for the last thirty-eight years.

Will I be a widower and grieve Molly's loss for years to come? I don't want to be old and alone for my final years.

Will I prematurely rush into a relationship, afraid of loneliness and emptiness?

Guilty thoughts assault me that I haven't loved Molly the way she desired and deserved over our twenty-five years together. Maybe I am better alone since I am such an introvert and enjoy seclusion and independence.

My heart seems to be such a small love tank, especially when compared to Molly's huge, loving heart. It seems so little, so easily satisfied, that brief interactions with family and friends quickly fill it.

Dear God, please help us. You've got to heal Molly; I don't know how I can manage life without her.

Molly slowly woke up in the recovery room.

She was pale and looked far older than her seventy years. Molly seemed so frail; I wondered when she started looking this way. Her eyes slowly fluttered open, and she stared at me with her warm brown eyes.

Molly gave me a small quizzical smile. "How did my surgery go? What did Dr. Greer tell you?"

Emotion rolled over me, waves pounding on the shore, and tearfully I told her, "He said he was very sorry, but there's nothing he can do to help you. The cancer is everywhere in your abdomen. There are tumors in the omentum, the ovaries, the liver, pancreas, and all over the peritoneum."

Molly didn't cry; she wasn't visibly upset. She seemed to accept the hard journey ahead of her. She had always been less emotional than me. I knew part of that was her peaceful temperament, but mostly it was her great faith in God, her loving Father.

"Isn't there anything they can do?" she quietly asked me, a quiver in her voice.

Choking back the tears, I could barely speak. "Well, he said they could give you very potent chemotherapy to try to slow the cancer. But when I asked him if it would destroy it, he replied, 'That would be a miracle.'"

Beginning to sob, I reached out and took Molly's hand, desperately wanting to climb in bed and wrap her in my arms. But I couldn't because I didn't want to hurt her so soon after surgery. I struggled to comfort her and encourage her. I was such a mess.

Her tears overflowing, Molly then consoled me and reminded me, "Tim, it's okay. I am not afraid. God is on the throne. He has good plans for me, and no matter what happens, He's in control, and He will take care of us."

We knew God could heal Molly in an instant or over many months, with or without medical treatment. We knew God loved her dearly and had plans for her life. We didn't want Molly to die; we wanted her to live and tell everyone that her loving Father had done a miracle and healed her. We earnestly tried to keep focusing on Him and not on the terrible storm swirling around us, threatening to overwhelm us with fear, doubt, and discouragement.

Yet, we felt we shouldn't focus all of our hopes and prayers on her healing, constantly petitioning God for our miracle. We could have focused on pursuing the "present" of a miracle healing from Jesus, but instead, we focused on the "presence" of the healer, Jesus, our Lord. In Him, we move, we live, and we have our being. In Him, we have abundant life, whether here on this temporal earth or with Him for eternity.

> *Then they cried to the LORD in their trouble, and he saved them from their distress. He sent out his word and healed them; he rescued them from the grave. Let them give thanks to the LORD for his unfailing love and his wonderful deeds for mankind. (Ps. 107:19–21, NIV)*

9

WHAT DO WE DO
WITH KATIE B?

SEPTEMBER 21, 2018

*K*atie had been in a slow mental and physical decline over the last twenty years. We were very concerned about her future and guardianship issues, so we met with Joann Wood, a lawyer who specialized in estate planning. Fortunately, Joann said we had all the proper legal documents in place to take care of Katie and place her in a nursing home if necessary. She encouraged us to find a suitable facility as soon as possible so that Molly could help Katie with the transition into her new home. She believed that dealing with one crisis at a time would be far easier for all of us.

On the way home, Molly asked me, "How can we do this to Katie? Our home is all she's ever known. She tries so hard to be independent, but she really needs me. It will break her heart if we place her in a nursing home before she is ready to go. Don't forget; I believe the Lord is going to heal me. I am not going to die!"

"But, Molly," I argued, my eyes filling with tears, "I am praying and hoping with all my being that you don't die, but we need to be ready for whatever happens to you. I think Joann may be right. How can I possibly take care of you and Katie if things don't go the way we hope? Taking care of her has become far more difficult these last several years. I have no idea how we can do this."

"Tim, God will make a way even if we can't see the path. He has always helped Katie and showed me what to do for her. We have to trust Him to show us His plans for her."

As we continued home in silence, my thoughts drifted back to how far Katie had come since graduating from high school. She moved into our basement apartment, and Molly continued pouring her life into Katie, trying to help her be as independent as possible. Molly even found her a small part-time job stocking shelves at JOANN Fabrics. Katie had always been very artistic, even as a child. She loved to do drawings and arts and crafts. Molly taught her to cross-stitch with only one hand, and it became a wonderful creative outlet for her. Over many years, Katie stitched dozens and dozens of beautiful messages that became treasured gifts for many family members and friends.

Molly encouraged Katie to keep a journal and write to the Lord every day about her frustrations, her hopes and dreams, and her prayers. She would also write about how the Lord spoke to her and encouraged her, and helped her. Katie also loved to write notes to encourage people. It was a humbling experience to get a card of encouragement from someone whose life was so hard. Everyone treasured those special notes, for they reminded us of God's faithfulness in using the broken and the weak to encourage even the strong.

Russ Dobson, an old church friend who has known Katie since she was a little girl, remembers her with great love:

"As I have grown older, I have come to realize that with age come aches, pains, and physical hindrances. Yet, they pale in comparison to my dear Katie B. When I see her, talk to her, make her smile, and see her faith in a Father who has not chosen to heal her, I see a level of faith and courage that is inspirational. I look at Katie and see that though her body and mind do not work the way she wishes, I see someone the Father has perfected and is biding His time with until the day she bursts forth in all her magnificence. If Katie can keep going, despite her great struggles, I certainly can come through whatever struggles I face."

In the fall of 2010, we built a new apartment on the front of the house to bring Katie upstairs. Then, in the spring of 2011, she had a terrible fall in her living room and landed headfirst on the base of the piano bench. She ended up with two herniated discs in her neck that required spinal fusion surgery. The injury resulted in her having to use a wheelchair for the rest of her days.

After the operation, we couldn't leave her home alone anymore. Since Molly was teaching only two English classes, she started taking Katie with her. Katie would work in the school office, doing simple jobs for the staff. Molly was always so creative in helping Katie and finding ways for Katie to give and help others. Molly asked a dear friend, Niki Baker, to help Katie while she was at school. Niki found out about Katie's journals and was amazed at the fascinating things Katie had written over the years to encourage herself and others. Niki and Molly decided to publish a book about Katie's life and her words of encouragement. Niki did an excellent job working closely with Katie and finally self-published the book, *CHIN UP! Through Adversity Hope Lives*. Katie's very inspirational book has touched the lives of hundreds of people.

RECENT YEARS

After high school, Katie slowly started showing more signs of decline due to her regular epileptic seizures. As a result of hundreds of headfirst falls over the last thirty years, Katie's brain had been repeatedly traumatized. Over the last several years, her decline had accelerated. Her memory became very poor; she lost her ability to read, play most games, do crafts, and do her beloved cross-stitching. For many years I thought CTE, chronic traumatic encephalopathy, might be causing her decline. This disorder often afflicts athletes with brain damage due to repeated head trauma. CTE results in steady cognitive decline and premature death.

Katie's decline had become more and more challenging for Molly. She had retired a couple of years earlier to fully devote herself to Katie and volunteer at school and the CareNet Pregnancy Care Center. Molly tried to find ways to keep Katie active and involved by helping others. They were always working on projects helping family, friends, or charities. I am sure the Lord is particularly fond of Molly and Katie because they loved laying their lives down helping others.

In September, Caitlin Guild, a dear family friend of Katie's back in the 1990s, contacted us and offered to help us any way she could. She had always been a loving, caring friend of Katie's for many years until she moved to California with her family in 2003. Over the last ten years, Caitlin had become a professional caregiver helping the severely disabled and elderly at the end of their lives. When Caitlin heard about our great difficulty, she called and offered to help take care of Molly and Katie. We appreciated her offer, but we were unsure if we would follow the lawyer's advice and try to find a new home for Katie.

FAMILY WISDOM

The day after we visited with the lawyer, several of Molly's closest family members came to visit us for the weekend. Her brother Ron, sister-in-law Joanne, niece Megan, and her mother Marie had come to support us as we faced this great crisis. Saturday evening, we talked for a long time about our options for Katie.

Molly shared with them about her deepest desires. "If these are my final months to live, I want Katie to be with me. She needs me, and I need her. Moving Katie to a nursing home will be incredibly stressful for her. If she is under great stress, I will be under great stress trying to help her. Imagine how hard it will be for her if I'm no longer here to take care of her. I'm the only care provider she has ever known. She will also be leaving her home and the beautiful apartment that she loves. She would lose her independence and would have to live with people she doesn't know or trust."

After much discussion, Molly's family strongly encouraged us to keep Katie and Molly together as long as possible.

Molly's brother Ron pointed out, "It sounds like your friend Caitlin is the answer to your desires. She is not only an old friend you trust, but she has professional experience that would be a great help for you and Katie as you manage the challenges ahead."

After talking to them, Molly and I felt the Lord leading us not to divide our family in our time of great need. Instead, we needed to draw close together to love and support one another as never before. If Molly were to pass away, then Caitlin and I would take care of Katie until we could find a suitable nursing home for her. It seemed that this was the hand of the Lord in providing somebody whom we not only knew and trusted, but who was also a friend of Katie's who knew and loved her dearly. Caitlin was not only skilled in helping people with disabilities, but she also had many experiences helping people with end-of-life challenges.

I remember thinking, *How in the world am I going to do this? Life is hard enough just taking care of Katie with all of her disabilities, but how can I possibly take care of her while Molly is fighting for her life?*

For weeks we didn't know what to do, but then the Lord provided the answer. When I called Caitlin, she agreed to help us as soon as possible. Caitlin rejoiced that the Lord had directed her to serve us. She indeed was heaven-sent to us in our time of great need. In the months that followed, Caitlin proved to be an amazing caregiver and friend for both Molly and Katie B. Full of wisdom, loving compassion, and a heart to serve, Caitlin was a great blessing for our family.

Be anxious for nothing, but in everything by prayer and supplication, with thanksgiving, let your requests be made

known to God; and the peace of God, which surpasses all understanding, will guard your hearts and minds through Christ Jesus. (Phil. 4:6 NKJV)

10

JESUS THE HEALER

*I*t was very early Saturday morning, the sky showing a glimmer of dawn, but I couldn't sleep. I'd tossed and turned all night in a nightmare that wouldn't end. I still couldn't believe Molly's death sentence and didn't want to face the threats that were before us. Molly seemed to be stirring, and I wondered if her night had been as bad as mine.

I reached out to touch her shoulder, saying, "Are you awake?" and she turned over and responded, "Yes, I could hardly sleep." I held her tightly, not wanting to let her go, now or ever.

We talked about what Dr. Shah had initially said: "We'll give you one chemotherapy drug for three months and try to destroy as much cancer as we can. After that, you'll have surgery to remove as much cancer as possible from your body. Then we will start another chemo regime to destroy whatever cancer is left and drive it into remission."

Now Dr. Shah was telling us that because of the rapid growth of cancer throughout Molly's abdomen and internal organs, she needed three powerful chemotherapy drugs. The side effects were dangerous, having the potential to cause bowel perforations, high blood pressure, or hemorrhaging, in addition to severe damage to her liver and heart.

Dr. Azid, a cancer specialist at Johns Hopkins, recommended six months of this stringent chemotherapy every two weeks, but only to try to drive the cancer into remission. It wouldn't destroy the tumors. Molly would then go on maintenance chemo for the rest of her short life. Recurrence was certain.

"I can't believe this," I said. "All the doctors can offer you are very harsh drugs that won't heal you. They'll just slow the process of dying—no hope for a cure, no hope for life."

Molly was silent, looked at me, stared out the window, then looked back at me. She took a deep breath, was entirely still except for her eyes beginning to pool with tears, and shook her head side to side, very slowly.

"I don't want to do it. I don't want that poison in my body, hoping the medicine helps me survive a few extra months. You know how I hate drugs! I hate what they do to me. I hate how they make me feel." She had a quiver in her voice, but she was amazingly calm considering her fate. I could tell she was determined to do what she felt was best for her body.

Molly had always preferred living with pain to taking a pill. When she broke her leg and tore a calf muscle, the pain was so excruciating she grudgingly accepted morphine, only to have a terrible reaction. From that point on, she refused opioids and would only use Tylenol for intense pain.

"Remember what Dr. Brown said when I asked him, 'If you had my prognosis, what would you do?' He said, 'If I had your cancer, I would quit my practice, move to California, and spend my last months with family and my grandsons. I wouldn't undergo severe chemotherapy treatment.'" She paused. "Tim, I feel the same way."

Her eyes filled with tears again, and her voice trembled. "If I'm going to die, I don't want to be so sick that I can't enjoy my last months with my family and friends. If I only have a few months, I want to live as fully as I can. I want to love my children, my grandchildren, and my dear friends. I want to abandon myself to Jesus, who promised me abundant life here and now. I want to put my absolute trust and hope and faith in Jesus, my healer. If it's going to take a miracle for chemo to kill all my cancer, I want the miracle of Jesus healing me without any chemotherapy."

Shaken, I asked her, "Are you sure? Are you certain? Chemotherapy is the only hope the doctors are offering you to extend your life."

"I am absolutely certain. I don't want to go down that road. All my life, I've avoided taking drugs. I want to live naturally, the way God created me. Why would I face the greatest struggle of my life taking horrible drugs instead of trusting in the Lord?" She gave me a little smile as her face brightened with absolute assurance. "I have an incredible win-win opportunity. If Jesus wants to take me home—to live with Him and my loved ones forever—then that's wonderful, and if He wants to heal me, that's even better. I'll be able to tell everyone what Jesus did for me."

Tears started streaming down my face. "Well, that's easy for you to say. I'm not ready for you to leave today or tomorrow. It's too much for me to bear, too great a loss if you go home. How will I ever manage without you?" All I could do was wrap my arms around her and hold her so close she could never leave me.

After a good cry, we dried each other's tears, and I cried out to the Lord, "Jesus, we surrender to You. Do with us what You will. You are on the throne. You are in control. You have a plan for us; show us what to do, and give us the strength to glorify You through the hard days ahead."

Then we recited one of our favorite Scriptures: *"Bless the Lord, O my soul; and all that is within me, bless His holy name! Bless the Lord, O my soul, and forget not all His benefits: who forgives all your iniquities, who heals all your diseases, who redeems your life from destruction"* (Ps. *103:1–4 NKJV*).

We'd both been living in dread as we faced the daunting chemo protocol ahead of us, which was to have started on Monday. Once we put our trust in the Lord instead of hoping for a medical miracle, we had peace, joy, and hope, even in our sorrow. We chose to rest in Him and His purposes for Molly's life.

We focused on our Lord Jesus, and the peace of God that passes all understanding filled our hearts. All those we told about her decision were supportive, especially our family. Some, like Maria, our daughter-in-law, were very concerned at first, not knowing that many people who rejected chemotherapy still found healing. All our closest loved ones agreed that we must rest in the hand of the Almighty and watch Him do His mighty deeds. I gained such peace about her decision after being torn between treatment options and struggling with my faith.

I didn't know if Molly would be healed of cancer or pass on to be with Jesus. But I knew that Christ the healer had plans for our lives for good and not evil, to give us a future and a hope. I knew with a certainty that He ordains our steps.

> *For I know the thoughts that I think toward you, says the Lord, thoughts of peace and not of evil, to give you a future and a hope. Then you will call upon Me and go and pray to Me, and I will listen to you. And you will seek Me and find Me, when you search for Me with all your heart. (Jer. 29:11-13 NKJV)*

11

BEAUTIFUL BETHANY BEACH

SEPTEMBER 29, 2018

*F*riends and family urged us to get away to make beautiful memories while we could and focus on something other than cancer. The last four weeks had been like being on a raft in a storm-tossed sea, often plummeting in fear and then soaring in faith.

We decided to go to Bethany Beach, a small family-friendly beach community near Ocean City, Maryland. I had great memories of vacationing there with my family fifty years ago, and so had Molly with her young family.

To ease Molly's discomfort, I'd made a comfortable bed for her in the back of the SUV, where she snuggled like a squirrel in a bed of leaves. Over the next three hours, she enjoyed looking up at the endless blue sky and the floating white clouds. She praised the Lord and thanked Him for better days ahead.

We left cancer behind as we talked and listened to a couple of great books on the way that ended up changing our perspective and our lives. We were amazed at various stories of God's miraculous intervention and answers to prayer. Dr. Bernie Siegel's book, *Love, Medicine and Miracles*, was fascinating.

"It's amazing to me what the doctor witnessed," I said. "How could so many cancer patients die despite the best chemo and surgery treatments? And then, on rare occasions, a few patients, with great hope and faith, refused treatment and got better. They experienced the healing power of God and the power of the body to heal itself."

Molly exclaimed, "Tim, this is just what I am doing! I am committed to living life with great hope and faith. I'm trying to do all I can with a radical diet, exercise, and essential oils. I am also abiding in the Lord as never before in prayer, worship, thanksgiving, and communion with the Holy Spirit."

EXPECTATIONS VERSUS EXPECTANCY

In *Hope Beyond Reason*, Pastor Hess shared how he had to change his perspective to help him survive his acute myeloid leukemia, several near-death episodes, and a prediction that he probably had only one month to live. He learned to have a high expectancy in his relationship with Jesus and not put any expectations upon the Lord. Pastor Hess knew Jesus loved him and was in complete control. After a six-month battle for his life, God miraculously healed him of cancer. Even more astounding, he also survived a ruptured appendix that doctors could not remove that should have killed him. Today, he has a tremendous testimony of God's faithfulness and His miracle-working power.

"I really like what he is saying," said Molly. "All my life, I have experienced unfulfilled expectations that I put upon my parents, my kids, and my first husband. When they didn't meet my expectations, I was disappointed in them."

"Yeah, me too," I replied. "It makes you lose faith and trust in people you love. I see how I am tempted to no longer fully trust God when I have unmet expectations."

"I don't want to live in false expectations anymore," said Molly. "I can't expect the Lord to heal me; instead, I want to lean on Jesus as never before in hope and great expectancy that He will accomplish

His purposes in me and through me. Live or die, I want Him to be glorified. I don't know what His plans are for me, but I know they are good and not evil. All I can do is live one day at a time, trusting Jesus to take care of me."

When we arrived at Bethany Beach, we were amazed that we had the entire beach practically to ourselves. We read uplifting books to each other for hours and took long walks along the beach. We delighted in the warm breeze, the clouds dancing above the ocean, the roar of the waves, the tangy smell of saltwater, and the seagulls floating on the wind crying out as if worshiping the Lord. God was restoring our souls and bodies as we walked in His presence and glorified the Creator of such beauty.

Then, very early one morning, we were walking on the beach, praying and worshiping the Lord while the sun rose over the waves. A lady came up behind us and said, "I smell patchouli oil. Are you wearing patchouli oil?"

I was astonished. "Yes, but I'm amazed that you can smell it out here. I have been rubbing this oil on my wife, trying to destroy her cancer."

I had been anointing Molly with various essential oils for the last several weeks, including patchouli, since they are supposed to help destroy cancer. I then told her Molly's story and why we had come to the beach.

She told us her father had recently died an excruciating death while fighting brain cancer. "I don't think the chemotherapy helped much at all. It made his last weeks miserable. I'll never do chemotherapy. It's a horrible way to die."

We thanked her and continued walking along the shore, worshiping the Lord, and marveled that the Lord had sent this woman to encourage us. We felt that we were in the presence of the Almighty. Molly grabbed my arm. "Tim, I believe the Lord has just spoken to me:'You shall not die but live, and give Me all the glory!'" We rejoiced and thanked Him for His wonderful promise, His love, and His faithfulness.

Molly had done extraordinarily well over the weekend. She had her energy back, walking over twelve thousand steps each day, three times more than she had been able to do over the last three months. Molly was full of joy and life. Her abdomen was not filling up with fluid so rapidly, and she had little pain. God was healing her before our eyes. We rejoiced that our God is so good!

> *The right hand of the Lord is exalted; the right hand of the Lord does valiantly. I shall not die, but live, and declare the works of the Lord. (Ps. 118:16 NKJV)*

12

IT'S ALL ABOUT LOVE

OCTOBER 2018

*W*e were blessed to have a great, loving family. Unfortunately, four of our children and our six grandchildren all lived out of state and could not provide much in-person support. Their phone calls and letters of encouragement were deeply appreciated, even though they could only visit a few times. Yet, we were also blessed to have four young families in our church who considered us their church grandparents. Their fifteen children called us Grandma Molly and Grandpa Tim. They were a tremendous support and encouragement for us. We loved them dearly.

Many times Cristina McOmber and her four young children would come to visit Molly. They wanted to bless her and love on her but often left in tears, touched by Molly's love and faith. Molly loved to remind her family and friends that God had a plan, He was in control, and He was good.

One time Cristina visited without the kids so she could have some quality time with Molly. They spent a long time sitting on the couch reminiscing and sharing heart to heart.

"Molly, I need to thank you for your friendship and love for the past thirteen years. You and Tim were one of the first to open your home to me. I was a foreigner who barely spoke the language. You have been present and very involved in my life from the very beginning."

"Well," replied Molly, "when I heard that there was a new girl in the church from Colombia, my heart went out to you. I knew how hard it was for my boys' wives, Maria and Ariadna, when they first came to America from Colombia."

"Then you and Tim did our premarital counseling and took the time to share your experiences and wisdom before we got married. When things looked like maybe they might not work out, you were encouraging and never shy when warning us about future problems."

"We all have to learn the hard way," Molly reminded her, "that God didn't make marriage to make us happy. He designed marriage to make us holy."

Laughing, Cristina replied, "And to make babies! Every time we dedicated one of our children, Anna, Zach, Nathan, and Abigail, you were there, representing more than a friend, but family. You have always taken the time to help my children. You even helped them make and decorate their own birthday cakes."

Molly laughed, "Of course, I did! I love your kids, and I love birthdays. I so enjoyed coming to your house to visit them and do lots of fun projects, especially the messy ones you couldn't handle on your own."

"I can't tell you how many times you rescued me by watching the kids so I could take a shower, clean my bathrooms, or go shopping. Having so many little ones often left me exhausted and with no free time."

Nodding her head, Molly agreed. "I remember those hard days when my kids were so young. There were so many things I needed to do that I often felt overwhelmed. Having the help of a friend means so much."

"By being present and loving my children from the very beginning, you have been such a great grandma, Molly. But what I really appreciate about you has been your love. You have been another mother to me. Your gentleness and kind but firm words of encouragement have shaped my life and the way I see motherhood. You are the woman of God I aspire to be: going the extra mile, being generous, and listening without trying to fix anything. I am so grateful for you, and so is my family. I have always admired you; your resourcefulness and perseverance and patience have taught me not to give up but to find a way."

Tears filling her eyes, Cristina's voice quivered as they embraced. "I love you, Molly. Please don't leave us."

"Believe me, I don't want to leave you or your family," replied Molly, wiping the tears from her face with her sleeve. "I believe the Lord has told me He will heal me. We just need to trust Him with all our hearts. He has a plan."

❄ ❄ ❄

Candice Zeiler also thought of Molly as her spiritual mother who dearly loved her, Gavin, Sammy, and Audrey. Since Molly enjoyed getting cards and letters from friends, Candice decided to write her a note of appreciation:

"Dear Molly, you have been such an extraordinary lady, both to my family and myself. I first met you at church. I had been helping with Riversong Christian Daycare and doing some decorating for the church, and so had found myself hanging out at church more often than not. Tim had mentioned to me that perhaps you and I could help each other. You could babysit my son Gavin, and I could watch Katie on days that you needed to go to work at KCA. I thought that sounded like a great idea, so that was when our relationship started. Then you often offered to watch Gavin even when you didn't need help with Katie. And Gavin, he loved spending time with you and

Tim, and started calling you guys Grandma Molly and Grandpa Tim. Every time Gavin came to your house, he had a list of things he looked forward to doing with you. Gavin often couldn't wait for me to leave so that he could have Grandma Molly all to himself!"

"Then I had two more children, Sammy and Audrey. All three of my children looked forward to spending time with Grandma Molly, especially when you invited them over regularly to help make cookies. Making cookies with you became such a special time for my children. You even let them help you wash the dishes. They loved this part just as much. Boy, did you know how to make children feel loved: it was merely by spending time with them."

"You were one of the people in my life who I found so easy to get to know. I felt like we were instant friends; we just connected. Maybe it was our similar Pennsylvania roots, but I think we shared a lot of commonalities. We both liked to cook and do crafty things, we both cared about simplicity in life, we both enjoyed natural foods and remedies, we both enjoyed teaching, and we both loved children. I learned a lot from you, and I know you felt like a mom figure to me."

"You always opened your home to me, no matter how busy your schedule. You never turned me down for babysitting or getting together for any reason. I will always remember you saying, 'I can do that!' I have kept that truth for my own life, as in merely remembering how selfless you were and praying that I would do the same for the people in my own life. And you said it with such a genuine spirit. You never hesitated; you always meant it. *Always* meant that you could do that for me, *always* meant that you loved me, and *always* meant that you were praying for me. You were in my corner!"

"You always tried to understand my situations, tried to offer care and support, and genuinely prayed for me. Remember that time when my family and I left the church for two years? You were one of a few people who continued to reach out to us from the church, hoping we would return. Recently you reminded me that you had never stopped praying for my family and me."

"You will always hold a special place in my heart and the hearts of my children. Even in your difficult days, you still want us around you. You always take the time to speak into my life, even when I intended to come and bless you that day. You encouraged my children to live for the Lord and told Gavin that he would become a great man of God. Your incredible impact on our family will be felt forever. We love you, Grandma Molly."

ALL ABOUT LOVE

Fortunately, we had a great home church, Our Father's House Assembly of God, where many people loved us dearly and helped us. Friends from Molly's school, The King's Christian Academy, and Community with a Cause Church were also very supportive and provided meals and visits.

Over many months we never had to cook a single meal. Ladies from our church would also come to pray and worship with Molly, lifting her closer to the Lord. One of our dearest friends, Russ Miller, a very talented songwriter/singer, would perform house concerts for a few close friends and us. His incredible music filled our living room with love and lifted our spirits:

There's a place that I know where the poor people go
And they find what the world's dreaming of
It's not really a place, it is more like the Face
Of a Man who is All About Love

I don't care...who or where
Time to share...All About Love
Day or night, black or white
It's all right...All About Love

He still lives here today and He looks for a way
To reach down to His child from above
Won't you give Him a try, if you don't you will die
And He'll cry, 'cause He's All About Love.

—Russ Miller, "All About Love"

SENTENCE OF DEATH
October 15, 2018

In the early stages of Molly's sickness, we had difficulty keeping all of our friends and family up-to-date with the latest news. A friend told me about a great website, CaringBridge, where we could post photos and messages about Molly's condition and challenges. It was open to anyone who wanted to follow our life-or-death journey. Here are a couple of entries that Molly wrote:

I continue to fight for health and life. I have good days, and I have some bad days when I am in pain and very tired. The fluid in my abdomen continues to increase, so the doctor will remove it again this Wednesday. Hopefully, the pain in my back and rib cage will significantly lessen as it did the last time the nurse drained the fluid.

I read this passage recently and took it for my own. It is Paul's testimony about the faithfulness of God to him, and though I have read it many times over the years, this time, it really spoke to me in my current circumstance. I have felt "the sentence of death." I have admitted we cannot "rely on ourselves, but on God." I have recognized that "you help us by your prayers" and that we have had "gracious favor granted to us in answer to the prayers of many." Thank you so much for standing with us, lifting us up to the Lord.

We do not want you to be uninformed, brothers and sisters, about the troubles we experienced in the province of Asia. We were under great pressure, far beyond our ability to endure, so that we despaired of life itself. Indeed, we felt

we had received the sentence of death. But this happened that we might not rely on ourselves but on God, who raises the dead. He has delivered us from such a deadly peril, and he will deliver us again. On Him, we have set our hope that He will continue to deliver us, as you help us by your prayers. Then many will give thanks on our behalf for the gracious favor granted us in answer to the prayers of many. (2 Cor. 1:8–11 NIV)

TWIN GIFTS OF LIFE—MOLLY'S POST ON CARINGBRIDGE

October 18, 2018

Yesterday was a great day for me. I had to be at the hospital two hours early for my appointment, so my friend Peggy drove me there, brought me a book of hope-filled stories, and read it to me. When the nurse came in, she encouraged me in my no-chemo decision, confirmed all my alternative weapons, and printed out some pages from a holistic treatment center that she knew was being successful. When I got to the surgery room, another nurse said, "You smell really good! Is that patchouli?" I was delighted. She sounded just like the stranger on the beach. They both gave me much more encouragement and affirmation. So far, all the warnings I was given about people who would pressure me to take the standard treatment have been unfounded. Thanks to all of you who love me!

He drained two liters of fluid from my abdomen, much less than we expected. I came home greatly relieved and slept through the night without back pain.

What could be better? That's not a rhetorical question. The answer is that today, our daughter Christi delivered two healthy, beautiful twin daughters. They are Caylee Rose and Jaynee Nolana. We are all overjoyed at the restoration and joy in the Jones family. Congratulations to Christi, Chris, and Alexis!

Thank you, Jesus, for the gift of life for me and my precious granddaughters.

ABUNDANT LIFE

All of life is mud and marble. We have seasons of great blessings and seasons of great sorrow. One of the lessons Molly and I learned over the years is that the Lord never promised us a life without pain. Instead, He promised to always be with us in the midst of our trials and our suffering. He promised to fill us with His presence so that we can choose to be joyful despite our painful circumstances.

For many years after the death of Brianna, Christi and Chris were unable to have more children. Finally, six years later, the Lord not only blessed them with one baby, but He abundantly blessed them with two beautiful girls!

Even during our great crisis, we were often filled with abundant joy as the Lord poured His love and blessings into our lives.

> **I have come that they may have life and that they may have it more abundantly. (John 10:10 NKJV)**

13

MOLLY'S KCA TESTIMONY

NOVEMBER 16, 2018

*T*he Lord gave me a great idea one day. I knew Molly always loved encouraging her students to trust in the Lord no matter how difficult their challenges.

"Molly, what do you think about sharing your testimony with the students at King's Christian Academy?"

She was quiet for a moment, then replied, "I'm not sure I can do that. I'm so tired, and it's hard to think clearly. Let me pray about it and see what the Lord says."

By mid-November, cancer was slowly draining Molly's life away. She needed to have the fluid removed from her abdomen more frequently, which meant the cancer was spreading. She continued losing weight and was getting weaker. But, after reflection, Molly decided to share her testimony of faith at a chapel service at her old school.

"Tim, the Lord encouraged me to tell my story of surrender. I've had some very hard seasons, but God has always been faithful. Maybe it will help them overcome the challenges in their lives. I want to encourage them to always look to the Lord in their time of need and suffering. I believe something beautiful can come out of this hard season."

The Lord blessed Molly when Megan, her niece, visited for several days. She has always been very loving and helpful with Katie, and as an English teacher, she helped Molly a great deal. Together they worked on the testimony, making it as clear and compelling as possible. Molly had taught public speaking for many years and was an accomplished public speaker. She wanted this speech to be the best of her life and have the most significant impact.

We arrived at KCA on that cold, windy day in November for the chapel service. As we slowly walked down the hall, Molly gripped my arm. "Tim, I'm not sure I can do this. I feel so weak and overwhelmed. I can barely walk down this hall. I need to stop and rest. I don't think I can do this."

I knew how hard she had worked on the speech and how important her message was. "Molly, I know this is very hard for you. Let's take a few minutes to recover and ask the Lord to help you. The Lord has promised that even though your flesh and heart may fail, He will strengthen you."

After a few minutes of rest, she rallied, and we entered the gym full of three hundred energetic, noisy upper-school teenagers who filled the bleachers. Molly loved this age group and had taught them for over twenty years. The chapel service always started with several worship songs before the message. I will never forget the look of amazement and delight on Molly's face when the very first worship song was all about surrendering to the Lord. She stood up and waved her white flag and joyfully worshiped the Lord as she surrendered to Him once again. When she was weak, He was strong. The joy of the Lord was her strength. When she started speaking, she was no longer weak and frail; she was now energized and full of life.

MOLLY'S KCA TESTIMONY

If your strength is made perfect in weakness, you will see His strength on display today.

I taught literature for many years, and literature is often depicted as a journey because we all begin at birth, and we have long journeys or short journeys. I'm going to share mine with you. I am going to begin at the very beginning of my life because I want you to get the whole picture of who I was and who I am now...

So now I am on a new episode of my journey. It may well be my last since I have stage 4 abdominal cancer, and I was given no real hope for survival. At first, the doctor said this is an incurable type of cancer. Despite treatment, it always recurs. The doctors offered six months of powerful chemotherapy using three different drugs. After six months, they would reevaluate to see if I would be a candidate for major surgery. I knew only a miracle could save me, so if I was going to need a miracle, I might as well fight cancer without chemotherapy. So we opted against that.

I am now doing everything I know to do, and many things friends have told me to do. They keep sending me emails saying, "Why don't you try to do this?" I am not complaining. I am so grateful that people care enough for me to do that. I am not doing the chemotherapy, but I am fighting cancer with everything God is giving me. You know God made our bodies able to heal. All of you right now have cancer cells in you. Your immune system, your white blood cells, and your T cells are fighting cancer cells and destroying them. But sometimes, our body breaks down, and our immune system gets out of control. And that's where I am. I am doing what I can to build up my immune system by doing a far-infrared sauna every day. The doctor said, "How can you do that every day? Where do you go?" Oh, my neighbor has an infrared sauna in her basement. Really! Yeah, that's my God. Things like that are happening all the time.

Again, my expectations were to live a long life. My mother is nine-ty-two and is still delivering mail to the people in her apartment building. She is still escorting residents in wheelchairs to special events. So I expected to live a long life like she is. But those are expectations, and I don't know what's going to happen to my expectations. I am in a season again to reexamine my expectations and put my expectancy in Jesus. I suppose that I could go tomorrow. But, you know, so could you. I could live longer than my mother, which is my short-term goal.

But in either case, every day, I know that God is with me. He's going to give me grace and comfort as He always has. He's there all the time. He's going to lead my family if they have to handle my passing on to heaven. I'll be in glory, and they will be here taking care of each other. And He's going to lead them, and my expectancy is that He will lead me as I rejoin them as a wife and a mother instead of someone who is dependent and needs a caretaker. I surrender all that to You, Lord. I just give up. I give up. I wave the white flag. I accept whatever You have for me.

I have great support from all the members of my family. I also have a family here at King's Christian Academy, where I taught for two decades. I have a family at Community with a Cause. It's a small Methodist church that we are highly involved in and love. I have family everywhere, where we all have learned to love Him and trust Him, to praise Him, and to take care of one another. We are not here with expectations but expectancy. We are not outlining for God what He should do. We are looking to Him for what He will do because His plan is always better than ours. We know that God goes before us, and He loves us and is both willing and able to do great things beyond what we expect.

One thing that happens to you when you are suffering is that you have more time to spend with the Lord. I found that out in the hospital with Katie. I would sit there all day praying for Katie and my family. I was worshiping, listening to worship music and scripture on CDs. I would have the whole day to spend with the Lord. I had no responsibilities like cooking or taking care of things at home because my church family was doing that for me; it was the best of times and the worst of times. Now here I am in the same condition.

Again you are carrying me. Some of my friends are bringing me dinner; some of you are coming to sit with me. Hospice called me and asked me if I wanted to have a home companion come out and spend time with me so that I wouldn't be lonely. I said, "No, please. I just need a few minutes every day to be by myself." Please don't take that to mean that I don't want friends to come. You are the kind of people that readily come, and you know this already because you have done it. You come to my home, and I don't even get off the couch. I just snuggle up in my blanket and lie down on the couch and spend time with you. You have no expectations of me, and I have none of you.

One delightful thing that I have found in this season is just being present with the Lord. I do this in my sauna a lot, and I do it all the time. I call on the Lord, and I come to know Him and the Father and the Holy Spirit in a deeper, more profound way. When I am weak like I am right now and I need a Father, I call on Him, and He wraps me in His arms. He is my Father. He loves me. When I need clarity, when I need to talk to the Lord, He talks to me. I go to Jesus. He's my go-to person. Because He talks like a human being, He knows me, and He speaks my language, and I can ask Him anything. He's my brother.

When I need power and strength to get through the day, the Holy Spirit comes. He always comes. He delivers me. But, if you want to be delivered, the only way to do it is to surrender. So I'm appealing to you today: whatever you're doing, whatever you are going through, and even if you are going through one of those glorious times like I was when I got out of college, you must surrender. Just surrender; just give up because He loves you, and He's waiting for you. And the last thing I want to say is thank you very much.

❄ ❄ ❄

After Molly finished speaking, you could have heard a pin drop. She was so soft-spoken the students had difficulty hearing her speak. They had become very quiet and attentive. It was remarkable. The gym—once so noisy and loud—had become very still. Everyone strained to hear her every word. Her testimony was so compelling, so powerful. Teachers later told me they had never seen the students so silent and attentive. When Molly finished, many students came to Molly in tears asking for prayer and encouragement in their season of great pain.

Molly's message was so moving that Pastor Lanny asked her to share her story on a Sunday morning. Her story had a profound impact on the congregation. Everyone was deeply touched and moved by her simple faith and total confidence that God was in control despite her prognosis. "Molly's Testimony" was recorded and posted to the church's YouTube channel. Soon, it went viral as hundreds of people were encouraged and challenged by Molly's surrender to God and her total assurance. She was certain that God was on the throne, He was in control, He had plans for her, and He was good!

> *Delight yourself also in the Lord, And He shall give you the desires of your heart. Commit your way to the Lord, Trust also in Him, And He shall bring it to pass. (Psalm 37:4-5 NKJV)*

14

CELEBRATION OF LIFE

NOVEMBER 25, 2018

Molly continued to fight the good fight against the hideous disease within her. Friends encouraged us to get help from hospice since they provide excellent support, comfort, and quality of life to patients with terminal diagnoses. At first, we resisted because we thought hospice was for people close to death. Molly was especially resistant because she was certain she wasn't going to die but *live*. However, after meeting with the hospice nurse, we discovered that they would provide special assistance for us as we tried to cope with the enormous challenges ahead. We loved the goal of hospice: "You matter because you are you. You matter to the last moment of your life. We will do all we can, not only to help you die in peace but also to live until you die."

Our nurse, Janette, was sent by God to help us in our hour of great need. She was compassionate and loving as she helped Molly with her disease and pain management. Her wisdom and understanding of the challenges we faced were a lifesaving rope that we clung to in our hard days.

Unfortunately, by the end of November, Janette confirmed that the rapidly growing cancer was causing the increasing buildup of fluid in Molly's abdomen. It was now taking only about a week to make Molly look six-months pregnant. We had to go to the hospital every week for about three hours to have her abdomen drained. Janette encouraged Molly to have a port inserted into her abdomen to drain the fluid at home whenever needed.

I wanted to help Molly at home since her swelling belly caused her significant discomfort and back pain. "Molly, what do you think about Janette's recommendation that you put a MediPort in your abdomen so we can drain the fluid ourselves?" I asked.

She looked at me with sadness in her eyes. Frustrated, she replied, "You know how much I hate the chemotherapy port they put in my chest when at first we thought I was going to have chemotherapy. It's so uncomfortable and so unnatural. It hurts whenever someone hugs me or when the grandkids bump me."

"But Molly, every week, you're spending three or four hours going to the hospital to get your belly drained. We now have to do it more often. Remember Janette said some people have so much fluid buildup they have to get drained three or four times a week. We don't know how fast the cancer is spreading. Wouldn't it be better for you if I could drain the fluid at home whenever you want? Janette said it's easy for me to do and painless."

She looked dubious and pensive, her eyes closing slightly with concern. "Okay, let me think about it and pray for a while. I'm not sure I want to put another tube in my body. But anything I can do to help me with this discomfort and pain would certainly be a blessing." A few days later, she agreed to do the procedure.

The doctor removed the chemotherapy port in Molly's chest and installed a new MediPort in her abdomen. Janette was right. It took us a while to get over our anxiety about draining Molly's belly at home, but over time, it was so much better to have me take care of her at home than having to go to the hospital so often.

❄ ❄ ❄

When we first met Janette, she told us stories of families that were helped by hospice, including many people who had recovered and left hospice care. Molly loved the positive outlook that hospice was not just for the dying but also for the living. She was still confident the Lord was going to heal her.

I found one story Janette told us very intriguing. She once had a client who had entered into hospice care. Upon his death, the family had a celebration of life service for him. His elderly wife loved all the memorable stories family and friends shared about her beloved husband.

A few months later, the wife also entered hospice care with a serious life-threatening condition. She told her family, "I don't want to wait until I die for you to celebrate my life. I want to have a great party right now and enjoy your love and beautiful stories before I pass away."

The family was very resistant. "Mom, you're not going to die anytime soon; why are you doing this to us?"

But the mother was a very strong-willed woman, and the family finally relented and celebrated her life. It was an extraordinary moment for her and all of her family and friends shortly before she died.

The story intrigued me, and I thought it was a great idea. If Molly was soon going home to be with the Lord, why wait until the memorial service to celebrate her amazing life? She deserved to hear how much we loved her and how highly so many people thought of her. Pastor Lanny had encouraged me to hope for the best but prepare for the worst. So, without Molly knowing, I made arrangements to have a potluck meal after church on Thanksgiving Sunday to be followed by a celebration of her life. I invited our family, our church family, and Molly's friends at The King's Christian Academy to join us.

After the potluck meal, some of Molly's old friends from school started drifting into the eating area. At first, she was delighted to see them but wondered why they were coming to our potluck meal.

Finally, Molly confronted me in mock anger. "Tim Frink, what have you been doing behind my back? Why are all these people here? What's going on?"

With a sheepish grin, I replied, "Molly, your family, and your dearest friends want to tell you how special you are and how much your love for them and devotion to Christ have changed them forever. Just relax and be blessed."

We then spent the next two hours hearing many people share loving words and touching stories. Molly was deeply moved, especially by the heartfelt thanks from several of her old students. It was a remarkable experience for her to bask in the love of so many. Molly, ever so humble, tried to deflect the praise and was often overwhelmed to tears. Here are two great testimonies from two of Molly's dearest friends.

LINNEA RAWLINS

My thoughts about Molly, a woman of eternal significance made of steel and velvet. Molly is an amazing human being who I've been blessed with as my sojourner in life for the past twenty-plus years. Even though she is two months younger, Molly is the big sister that I never had. She is always, always, always there for me, so steadfast. I never have to worry about what she will think about me, or what my house looks like, or what I'm wearing. Molly never judges people like that. You can be you, and she honors you just as you are.

Known by many as the Energizer Bunny, Molly's always spearheading, leading, or involved in something, often behind the scenes. Here are only a few that I'm aware of that I can remember: speech contests at the fair, children's Christmas Eve plays, Thanksgiving services, National Day of Prayer at OFH, encouraging writers, VBS, SOAP studies, grandmothering, decorating the church for Christmas and putting it away, directing plays at KCA, making costumes for countless dramas, proofreading, making cookies for the marriage retreat, skits, Katie's church, leading prayer groups, and hospitality on Sunday morning. I remember when she directed Song of Survival, a play at OFH, and fell off a chair, seriously injuring her leg, but she kept on going to finish practice with ice on it. She later went to the ER and discovered her leg was broken! Although on crutches, our fearless leader managed to direct the show and even play the roles of a few who were missing, along with her own part! Molly is gifted and confident in so many areas, and the thought that any particular endeavor might be a flop doesn't enter that arena or hold her down.

Molly is my go-to person for practical help. She can make or fix anything, except when I asked her how to darn socks, and she referred me to YouTube. Last spring, when I secretly decided to wear my twenty-eight-year-old wedding dress to my seventieth birthday celebration, Molly was there when we pulled it out of the sealed box, inspected it, and I tried it on. For days, she patiently worked on the stained bustle bow and also agreed to make a memory book containing the pictures and thoughts sent to me by friends. When I changed the plan late in the game and decided to put together a slideshow of our New Zealand trip, Molly agreed to make it happen even though she had no experience in that arena. Whenever I needed a quick proofreader for any words related to this event or any other project I was working on, she responded immediately, and I knew it was right...such a good feeling when an English teacher has done her magic on your work!

I love that Molly always has time for you. When I stop by for a visit just to catch up, we always end up talking for hours. Hospitality is her lifestyle. She warmly welcomes people into her life and home. There's always food available like she was expecting you, and she seems to whip up something delicious in no time. Molly can make anything from scratch in minutes, fitting it in alongside a game or puzzle with Katie. Her relationships are healthy and genuine with so many in our community. She is a Proverbs

31 woman in so many ways, but I especially appreciate that strength and honor are her clothing, she opens her mouth with wisdom, and the teaching of kindness is on her tongue.

One day Molly, Katie, and I went to DC to visit Virginia Mayer in the hospital. Molly volunteered to drive if I would navigate. All went well until we were on our way home. Roadwork and detours didn't jive with GPS, so the navigator was lost in the jungle for an hour until we finally saw the Capitol. While I was panicked and so sorry that I'd locked Molly in this stressful now-rush-hour traffic, she laughed, never blaming me amid the frustration.

I'm so grateful that Molly never gave up on Spence and me during our first ten years at OFH. She and Tim invited us on countless occasions, at least ten times for every one time that we accepted. Tim and Molly seemed to see some potential that God could see when we couldn't.

"Love suffers long and is kind, love does not envy; love does not parade itself, is not puffed up; love does not behave rudely, does not seek its own, is not provoked, thinks no evil, does not rejoice in iniquity but rejoices in the truth; love bears all things, believes all things, hopes all things, endures all things..." This is Molly and so much more in the eyes of her friend Linnea, who loves her bunches!

❀ ❀ ❀

Mary Wallace was an old friend who had known Molly since the early nineties. They were very good friends who had known each other very well.

Molly Frink, I would call you a lot of things, but I would never describe you as "nice."

"Nice" is defined as "pleasant, agreeable, or satisfactory." Being nice means you treat someone well, and you are polite. Niceness carries with it an indebtedness and obligation for reciprocal treatment. "Nice" has a public quality to it and requires thanks and recognition. The "nice" person *is externally motivated. It means you are doing things someone else requires of you and earns you their approval. No, I would never call you nice.*

I have known you for over thirty years. My oldest child is now thirty-seven-years old, which means my children have known you all of their cognitive lives. If they were present here today, they would each have stories of your many investments in their lives. They would tell of being free to be goofy as clowns in the early nineties when Micah wasn't yet old enough to walk. They learned to use laughter as an evangelistic outreach tool. They would talk about you directing plays where they were able to explore their thespian bent. They learned from you that theater art changes lives, both the performers' and the audiences. They would mention winning speech competitions under your excellent coaching, where they were able to share their core beliefs in the Right to Life movement in a public forum at a national level. They would talk about learning to appreciate and write poetry. You may remember Matthew's masterpiece poem, "Carrots Are Nasty Little Things." He was so proud of that poem being published. Writing poetry remained an important form of artistic expression for him. They would all tell about excelling in their chosen professions with stellar grammar, spelling, and writing skills, as well as the value of wordplay and the importance of diagramming sentences learned in your classroom.

At least one would report that you taught her that stripes and polka dots do indeed go together and that she shouldn't let anyone tell her differently. She would also say that you taught her to take hold of her differences and use them to her advantage in her unique skills. My children would also say that they learned the ability of an encouraging word to change a life, as their lives reflect many of the words spoken to them by you.

I have my own stories to tell about various adventures together. Some of my personal favorites involve your ingenious ways of allowing me to participate in multiple theater productions, working around my inability to memorize. In one production, my lines were all in a prop journal. In another, I taped my lines to the inside of a prop newspaper I was holding. It allowed me to do something I loved without my limitation excluding me.

No, I would never say that you are nice. I would only ever describe you as kind. Kindness is internally motivated love in action. Kindness looks for nothing in return. Kindness doesn't require praise and public recognition. Kindness isn't necessarily nice or popular, but holds the welfare of another above oneself and makes the hard choices for the sake of goodness.

We seldom see ourselves through the same lens those who love us see us. Today, it's your turn. It's often difficult to see the goodness that we hold and offer to others. You, my friend, have offered goodness every day that I have known you. You have exemplified the character of Jesus to my children and me consistently, and I am forever grateful.

I love you, kind Molly.

The words of love and appreciation from family and dearest friends especially moved us to tears. It was indeed an unforgettable experience for all, especially for Molly and me. I was amazed as I heard story after story of how Molly's life had touched so many people. It was a bittersweet experience for me. I was so thankful for Molly's sake that she could bask in the loving praise of so many. But my joy was tempered by the reality that, unless God intervened, I would soon be losing my incredible, extraordinary woman of love.

Charm is deceptive, and beauty does not last; but a woman who fears the Lord will be greatly praised. Reward her for all she has done. Let her deeds publicly declare her praise. (Prov. 31:30–31 NLT)

15

FAMILY VISITS

*O*ur kids, Katie and Kyle, and their young boys flew home for a brief visit at the beginning of December since they couldn't come home for the holidays. We had great fun with our three-year-old grandson Zebulon and his six-month-old brother Ezra. We treasured our time together, especially talking after the boys were asleep.

Katie shared her heart with us one evening. "You know, Molly, I will never forget 2018. First, Ezra was born in April, then you and Dad flew out to visit us, and then you got sick."

With a twinkle in her eye, Molly replied, "I was so eager to hold Ezra, my newest grandson, and visit with Zeb again. I love you and Kyle, but I especially love my grandbabies!"

Katie was delighted with the special surprise gift Molly had made for Zebulon. "Zeb absolutely loves the fabric 'quiet book' you made for him. It warmed my heart to watch the two of you spend hours snuggling on the couch working on the special activities on each page."

Molly had sown a book out of multiple colors of fabric with a different activity on each page. One page had strips of material that Zeb could weave together and button at the ends. Another had mittens that could be attached to a little boy. There was a page with a flat cutout of a person with multiple outfits and another with a tent and sleeping bag. Each page was full of creativity and challenged Zeb's development and imagination.

Katie seemed lost in thought as she remembered our time in Colorado. "You know, Molly, it wasn't apparent at the time, but I think you were fighting cancer when you visited us in July. Looking back, I can see something was different. You spent more time lying down on the couch while Zeb played around you. That was unusual for you, but you were still very engaged and made each of us feel special and deeply loved."

"Thank you, Katie. I remember often feeling very tired, but I didn't want to miss a moment with you and your precious boys. I love you all so much."

❄ ❄ ❄

Nate's wife, Maria, and Molly's niece Megan drove down from Philadelphia for a brief visit with Molly. Megan always had a special relationship with Molly. They both loved children, they both taught high school English, and they both loved Katie B. dearly. Megan shared a wonderful poem she had written, highlighting many of Molly's extraordinary gifts.

AUNT MOLLY'S POEM OF LIFE

I don't want to be melancholy, Aunt Molly,
But my rhymes aren't as fine as yours
My tribute not so astute
Therefore it is my humble guarantee
That these words will fall short of what you mean to me

You exude creativity, intelligence, love of nature
You know the meaning of words like nomenclature,
Acuity, ingenuity, munificence,
Your love for us always makes a difference

Though on some beliefs we might not concur
It is deeply true there never were
A family member who shows such interest
In my children's and my day-to-day existence
Every party, every family meeting,
You go beyond a simple greeting
To listen, confer, and share,
You show us that you really care

You're a flour maker, bread baker,
Caretaker, toy shaper
You tailored yourself a camel suit
And sewed us all Raggedy Anns to boot
You stitched Aunt Barb's wedding gown
You crafted your repertoire as a clown
One time, delighted, you said to me
How great the vest I was wearing would be...
...for your clown costume.
I gave it to you immediately!

Over the years, you have given me
Frogs in mugs and building blocks,
You've made us monkeys out of socks
Pieced quilts together to keep us warm,
Shared your stories from the farm.
You're my recipe and Home-Ec historian
You were your high school valedictorian

Resilient, Brilliant
Inventive, Strong
Patient, Direct
I could go on...

You'll roll down a hill with a grandkid
Step on your brothers' backs for a pyramid
Get nieces and nephews to do a magic show
There are so many memories, you know

Yankee Lake, Uno, and blueberries
Bananagrams, puzzles, and Scattegories
Reunions, 500, and bouts of laughter
I want you on my Trivial Pursuit team forever hereafter
You're the master of leftovers at Findley Lake
And we love your homemade ice cream cake

I've never heard you complain about what's wrong
You simply pick up and carry on

Your devotion to Katie B.
Always inspires me to be
A better parent and a better person
Of you, I want to be a version

I'll end it thus:
You are indelibly a part of us
And oh by gosh, by golly,
I'm so lucky that you're my Aunt Molly.

❄ ❄ ❄

Maria, Nate, and their three sons had come to the celebration of life service at Thanksgiving, but it was too hard for Maria to share her feelings publicly. Since English was her second language, she found it difficult to find the right words. Maria wrote this letter for Molly expressing her deep feeling of love and devotion:

"Dear Molly, when I think of you, I usually smile with nostalgia but also with satisfaction. You remind me of how generous, active, faithful, and strong a woman can be. You always looked relaxed but with a million things going through your mind. You could be playing games with Katie while at the same time making dinner, baking cookies, and correcting some papers from your students. What a great multitasker you are."

"We got to enjoy many of your amazing talents: your cookies and desserts (unbeatable), homemade quilts for the boys' beds, curtains for their rooms, hand-knitted sweaters, hats, and scarfs for them. You made amazing photo books for the boys on every birthday with their pictures and the best encouraging words."

"Your visits were the best, though you were like a hurricane. I usually had spent the whole day cleaning up and organizing, but hours after your arrival, the house was a complete mess. The boys were always asking Grandma Molly to read a story, or play a game, or do a new craft project, while planning the weekend with a very ambitious schedule."

"Your house was open for me from the first day we met, which was the day before my wedding with Nate. Since my family was in Colombia, South America, you loved me like your own daughter. You became an amazing mother-in-law, grandmother, and dear friend."

"There were times when I called you and said, 'Molly, I need you! Nate is out of town, and I have to play concerts every night this week.' Though you were a full-time high school teacher and had to take care of Katie B., you would turn your world upside down to help me. You and Katie B. would then drive four hours to my house, ready to take care of my boys. When everyone had gone to bed, it was our time to catch up, share stories about our families, to pray, to reflect on things I needed to learn about raising three boys."

"You have been in our audience for a week every summer, for thirteen years, as we performed at the Utah Festival Opera. You loved the shows, time with the boys, and having a special vacation week alone just with us. There are uncountable memories of joy and happiness from those days."

"I adore you immensely. You are a spiritual guide to me and an amazing doer of your faith, living your spirituality every day. Your life is a great example of love, patience, faith, and dedication. I feel honored to be one of your daughters. Your love and words of life will be part of me forever."

> *Love bears all things, believes all things, hopes all things, endures all things. Love never fails....And now abide faith, hope, love, these three, but the greatest of these is love. (1 Cor. 13: 7, 13 NKJV)*

Russ Miller singing "It's All About Love".

Molly and precious Katie B.

Marie Rose and her five children at Findley Lake.

Molly's son Andy & Ariadna Buonviri.

Tim & Molly with KC and Cristina McOmber.

Tim with the McOmber and Zeiler families.

Molly with Caitlin Guild our fantastic care-provider.

Molly with Christi, Caylee, and Jaynee Jones.

Molly holding Zeb Stamp.

Kyle, Katie, Zeb and Ezra Stamp and Katie B.

Molly & Katie Stamp.

Megan Cokonis, Molly and Maria.

Molly & Linnea Rawlins.

Pastor Lanny Clark & Pastor Jay Patterson.

16

ROSE FAMILY REUNION

Slowly, ever so slowly, Molly was leaving me. Ounce by ounce, pound by pound, she was wasting away. I was often brokenhearted, breaking down in tears as I watched her energy wane and her life become much more difficult. She spent more and more time lying on the couch in the living room, watching the fire dance in the pellet stove. Her eyes were often closed because she said it took too much energy to keep them open. Janette, her nurse, told me her passing away was not imminent but could happen at any time once cancer destroys a vital organ or a tumor blocks her digestive system.

Molly continued to be full of faith and assurance that she would not die but live and give God all the glory. I was less convinced that she would survive this horrible trial, but I was full of the assurance that God was in control, and He had plans and purposes I could not comprehend. I stood in faith that those who come to God must believe that He is God and that He is the rewarder of those who diligently seek Him. I didn't seek a reward from Him for Molly's healing and saving her life. But I knew that Jesus was my reward, and only with His strength could we triumph over such adversity. I often prayed, "Oh Lord, help me to be a rock in this very hard place."

My days were surreal. I was trying to live my days being positive, full of faith and assurance that the Lord was taking care of us. Then

I would be overcome with despair as I faced the reality that at any time, my precious Molly could be gone forever and leave us broken-hearted. I would be doing fine, taking care of the family when suddenly grief would overwhelm me. Grief became an old friend, a strange companion on my difficult journey. I slowly learned not to reject grief but embrace it, and embrace the pain until grief eventually released me.

I remembered a story in the book *Hinds' Feet on High Places*. Much-Afraid desperately sought to follow the Good Shepherd to the high places. Her two close companions were Sorrow and Suffering. In that season, my sorrow and suffering were always nearby to help carry me through the hard days and painful nights.

But there were also unforgettable moments of intimacy and connection with Molly that we had never shared before. Words were fewer and spoken less often but far more powerful. I came to treasure our times when I rubbed her feet twice a day for fifteen minutes to reduce the swelling. I also would anoint her swollen abdomen with essential oils. We spent the time worshiping and praying. Those times together each day were holy and sacred, profoundly intimate, and full of tender love. They were some of our most intimate times together because our spirits and flesh were joined in ways the mind cannot conceive. Truly we grew to love each other more deeply than I could ever imagine. Through great suffering, our love was being purified in the furnace of affliction.

A SPECIAL WEEKEND AWAY

As December progressed, I became increasingly concerned that we wouldn't be able to celebrate our twenty-fifth wedding anniversary on January 15. If Molly took a turn for the worse over the next six weeks, we would never enjoy our special day together.

The progression of cancer and its life-robbing impact upon Molly was very disheartening. I was genuinely hoping and praying for a miracle cure, but our future was so uncertain that I felt we needed to celebrate our anniversary while Molly was able.

I was convinced that Molly needed a special time away to leave our cancer-ridden world behind. So I decided to celebrate our anniversary on December 15, a month early. I made reservations at the Bavarian Inn in Shepherdstown, West Virginia, where we had our honeymoon twenty-five years earlier. It was a German chalet on the banks of the Potomac River. It was an extraordinary place for both of us, filled with treasured thoughts of our special time together. I even found a Christmas concert that weekend in a town nearby and made all the arrangements.

I was also so thankful for the wonderful celebration of Molly's life we recently had at the church. Molly loved it so much I decided that I wanted to give her family the same opportunity to have a surprise celebration of her life. I knew Molly's large family loved her dearly and would also want to spend an afternoon sharing stories and favorite memories with her. Loved ones from all over the country agreed to surprise Molly at her mom's retirement community in Harrisburg, Pennsylvania.

Molly thought we were stopping by to visit her mother on our way to the Sunday concert, since we hadn't seen her since September. You cannot imagine her surprise when her siblings and over thirty of her closest family members came to express their love. Someone had put together a poster board of old family photos that everyone enjoyed. Molly was delighted with the pictures and the warm memories they brought back. Megan shared the wonderful poem she had written about Molly's remarkable life. It was a wonderful day full of stories, laughter, and love, just what Molly needed.

THE DINER

Sunday morning, we went out for breakfast on a cold, dreary day with light rain falling. We found an old-fashioned diner—a polished countertop, bar stools, and worn-out linoleum. The nearly empty restaurant prompted extra attention from the waitress. She was a middle-aged lady, and her careworn face gave her a certain sadness. Her face reflected the frayed edges of a hard life.

But she was nice, had a pleasant smile, and was friendly. "Hello, my name is Sue. What brings you to Harrisburg this dismal day in December?"

I looked at Molly, wondering what to say, when she spoke up. "Tim and I are getting away to celebrate our twenty-fifth anniversary. We came to have a special time with my family since I have stage 4 cancer. My doctors have given me no hope for recovery. But my God has assured me that He loves me and that all things are possible. He is a good God, and He is in control. We are hoping and praying for a miracle!"

Shocked, Sue sat down beside me and sadly looked at Molly. "I am so sorry to hear you are so sick. I believe in God too, but I don't think He listens much to me. I've messed up my life pretty bad. I don't have no husband anymore, but it's okay since they both were more trouble than they were worth. My kids don't come around much, and I really miss my grandbabies. My boyfriend, he can be pretty hard living with. I keep telling him he's no good when he drinks too much."

Sue started crying softly. "I keep praying and asking God to help me, but nothing seems to change."

Molly tenderly smiled at her. "I lost a husband myself once, and I've had some pretty hard things happen in my life. But many years ago, I committed to following Jesus. He loves me, and I love Him. He wants the very best for my family and me."

Pausing momentarily, Molly asked, "Sue, do you have a church?"

"No, I used to go occasionally, but I usually work on Sunday mornings because there's most always a good crowd. Sometimes I watch TV preachers. But I don't often understand what they're saying."

"Sue, my hope is in the Lord and His promises to me that I found in the Bible. I believe that I will not die but live to give God all the glory."

I then spoke up. "Molly recently shared her life story at her school and our church, about how God helped her through many great difficulties. I think it would help you understand how Jesus can change your life too. You can watch it on YouTube. Just look up 'Molly's Testimony,' which she gave last weekend."

Sue smiled and nodded her head. "That sounds great. I really want to hear your story, Molly. I'll watch it as soon as I get off work."

Taking her hands, and with great compassion, Molly replied, "God loves you, Sue. He has special plans for your life, plans for good and not for evil. If you commit your life to follow Jesus, He will help you."

Taking a napkin, Molly wrote down John 3:16 and Isaiah 41:10. We then held hands and prayed with Sue, tears filling our eyes. After hugging her good-bye, Molly encouraged me to leave an extra-large tip. Though the day was still cold, wet, and dismal, the Lord had warmed our hearts with His love and joy.

Afterward, as we were driving to Hagerstown, we talked about our extraordinary experience. I was so proud of my amazing Molly—so weak in the flesh, yet so strong in the spirit—pouring out loving concern upon this hurting woman. I thought about our twenty-five years together and thanked God for such a rich blessing. I felt so honored to have been found worthy of her love and devotion.

Molly thoughtfully mused, "You know, Tim, if my sickness has been for no other reason than for this woman to hear the gospel and follow Jesus, then all the suffering will have been worth it."

When we finally arrived in Hagerstown for lunch, Molly wasn't feeling well and hardly touched her food. The travel and the cancer were taking a heavy toll on her. We had been looking forward to the Christmas concert by the Maryland Symphony Orchestra. Ariadna, our daughter-in-law, a very talented professional violinist, often performed with this orchestra.

Molly continued to feel bad as we made our way to our seats. Unfortunately, she felt worse and worse as the concert progressed. She started rocking back and forth in her seat, her arms wrapped tightly around her belly, groaning quietly. I had been earnestly praying for her ever since she started feeling bad. I so wanted this to be a special time for her.

I leaned over, pulled her close, and whispered to her, "Molly, how can I help you? Do you want to leave?"

She grimaced through clenched teeth. "My belly hurts so bad. I don't know if I'm sick or if it's the cancer."

Shaken, I asked, "Do you need to use the restroom? Do you need Tylenol?" Again, I asked, "Do you want to leave?"

She shook her head. "No, I don't want to make a scene. I don't want to bother everyone around us. I think I can manage until intermission."

She continued rocking slowly back and forth, praying, groaning softly and suffering. It was surreal. Beautiful, uplifting Christmas music soared around us, yet we both were hurting so badly. Molly was in great pain but did not want to make things difficult for others. She was always thinking more about others than herself. I was heartbroken for her, full of grief and despair for my poor Molly.

Finally, at intermission, we got up and put on our coats to leave. Two older ladies sitting behind us had been watching Molly in her extreme distress.

They were very concerned, and one of them asked, "Is your wife okay? Do you need help?"

Heartsick, I replied through clenched teeth, "No, she is not okay; she is very sick. We're leaving."

But inside, I felt like screaming, *No, she is not okay—she is dying! Please, can anyone help us? God, where are You? Please help Molly!*

Holding Molly close and half supporting her, we slowly made our way to the car and left with Molly curled up in the back in great pain. She fitfully slept the several hours it took us to get to the Bavarian Inn.

We checked in but skipped dinner and went right to our room. It had been such an exhausting day we went to bed early.

Molly's suffering had ruined my hopes for a special time together away from the curse of cancer. All I could do was pray for mercy and relief from the great pain for my poor Molly.

The next morning dawned bright, beautiful. God had answered our prayers! Molly felt much better, and so did I. We enjoyed a delightful breakfast. Molly savored each bite, especially the enormous chocolate-covered strawberry. We reminisced about our lives together over the last twenty-five years.

"I remember saying to my mother, when I first told her about you, that I wanted a man who knew God better than I did. I wanted a man of integrity who was faithful and kind, generous and strong. Mom said, 'Well, you're not going to find all of that in one man.' And I said, 'Oh yes, I am!'"

Delighted, I replied, "So, I was abundantly above and beyond all you could imagine or think?"

"That's right, and you were taller than I expected," said Molly, laughing. She paused and added, "We've had a lot of good laughs together."

I nodded my head and chuckled with her. "That we have."

Molly's eyes darkened. "And we've had a lot of sorrows and trials and challenges together. But it's all been good in the end."

"You know, Molly, all that adversity has made our lives ever so stronger and entwined. We're like two trees growing together side by side in the forest. Just one tree, standing alone in a field, would be that much weaker in the terrible storms of life. But because we have been growing together, our roots are tightly interwoven, and our canopies support one another. Our branches have become interlocked. There's great strength, stability, and power in that. It has helped us withstand the many great storms we have weathered over the years."

"Tim, remember how we struggled to blend our family? The girls didn't really want to be together in a new family. And the guys resented your girls because they were allowed to do things they weren't allowed to do. But we made it. We kept loving them and brought them all together. And now they love each other. And now they are no longer stepdaughters or stepsons. They're our children. I'm so glad my grandchildren are yours, and your grandchildren are mine. It's a wonderful thing."

Nodding, I replied, "It's God's amazing grace at work in our family. It took years to make it work. But through our love, faithfulness, and commitment to each other and the kids, we have a truly wonderful blended family. Our family is full of love, friendship, and delight."

"It's all because of the Lord," agreed Molly. "Over the years, we have seen almost all of our children start following the Lord. We keep praying for all of them." She reached across the table and grabbed my hands.

Closing her eyes, Molly prayed. "We thank You, Lord, because You've always been there for our family. You've always helped us, You have strengthened us, and You have guided us. We thank you, Lord!"

We finished our breakfast and made our way to the C&O Canal. We remembered the special walk in the snow we took along the canal many years before. Unfortunately, we only went a short way before Molly became too weary and needed to head back. Our trip home was quiet as Molly slept most of the hours away. I hoped she was dreaming fond memories from our many years together.

I had such an odd mixture of thoughts and emotions. The cold and the rain from the previous days had been blown away by a strong southerly wind. White clouds were racing like sailboats across the depths of the deep-blue sky. It was a warm, beautiful day full of promise for better days ahead, days without cancer, days without death. I listened to worship music all the way home, praying and worshiping my Lord, refusing to let this trial destroy my faith or my hope.

The weather over that weekend—cold, rainy, dark days followed by a warm, beautiful day—was a picture of our life. We had shared wonderful times, times of ministry, loving times with family, and times of peace and contentment, but there were many times of tears, pain, and suffering. It reminded me of Ecclesiastes 3:

> *There is a time for everything, and a season for every activity under the heavens: a time to be born and a time to die, a time to plant and a time to uproot, a time to kill and a time to heal, a time to tear down and a time to build, a time to weep and a time to laugh, a time to embrace and a time to refrain from embracing. (Eccles. 3:1–3 NKJV)*

17

CHRISTMAS 2018—
THE BITTER AND THE SWEET

Christmas was always one of Molly's favorite holidays. She loved having family come home for the special season. For many years Nate and Maria and their kids had celebrated Christmas with us. It was always a time filled with laughter, stories, fun, and games. Molly would spend weeks getting ready. She loved buying gifts for her grandchildren and everyone who came to visit. Molly also spent hours preparing a family calendar with photos of the kids and grandkids on each page. It was a labor of love that everyone treasured for years to come. She made various Christmas cookies by the dozens to give away and share with all of us, especially me. Molly always made sure Katie B. helped her with the preparations so she wouldn't feel lost in the bustle of the season.

We always had favorite games we thoroughly enjoyed, such as Gestures, Pictionary, and Sets. Katie especially liked the card game Golf, which was a lot of fun for her. We also played the card game Five Hundred for hours on end. It was similar to Bridge, though easier to play, and a family favorite from Erie. Over the last twenty-five years, we had played hundreds of games of Five Hundred with the boys. They usually won, which I found very annoying, but Molly didn't care. She just enjoyed being with them and having fun together.

Occasionally, I would question her card play. "Molly, why did you trump my ace? I had that trick won!"

Indignantly she would reply, "Listen, Frink, I have been playing Five Hundred for longer than you've been alive. I think I know what I am doing."

She was right; we both knew I was the weak link on our card team.

Molly would also devote hours to being with the grandkids and making them feel adored and special. Carlo and the twins, Paulo and Matteo, would no sooner arrive than they would clamor, "Grandma Molly, can we please play a game?" Each boy had a favorite game or craft project. She would play many games with them or let them help her make cookies and pies.

This year was different. Molly was so weak she couldn't do anything special before the holiday. She lay on the love seat in the den and offered suggestions as I worked on our annual Christmas letter and Christmas calendar. As Christmas approached, Molly continued to lose weight and become weaker. She had lost over thirty pounds and looked emaciated. It broke my heart to watch Molly slowly evaporate before my eyes like a fog on the bay. It wasn't just her flesh wasting away, but her spirit, her joy, the very essence of her being was disappearing before my eyes. She didn't talk much anymore. She was weak and tired, often suffering and in pain. She slept so poorly at night that she would sleep and rest with closed eyes throughout her days.

Daily, I would pray, often in great anguish, "Oh Lord, please ease her pain. Please stop her suffering and grant her a miracle recovery. Please give us a wonderful time with our family and a respite from this horrible disease."

We thanked the Lord that most of our family could join us for an exceptional Christmas together. Molly was especially delighted that Christi and her family drove from Michigan to be with us. She especially enjoyed snuggling with Christi's precious baby twins, Caylee and Jaynee. She said they were her favorite Christmas presents ever.

Since Christi couldn't come to the celebration of life service we'd had at Thanksgiving, she shared these thoughts with Molly one night:

"I recently heard a great quote, and I thought of you: 'You should aspire to have those characteristics in someone that you greatly admire.'

"Well, I greatly admire what an amazing educator you are. When I was really struggling to help Alexis cope with dyslexia, I could always turn to you for helpful insight and encouragement."

"I so admire how you are always careful to listen and slow to speak. You show such thoughtfulness by the way you listen to what people are sharing before offering up quick advice."

Molly chuckled. "I remember one time when you were in middle school that you indignantly responded to a word of correction. I think you said, 'I know a lot of things, and I know when I'm right!'"

Molly added, "You were pretty opinionated in those days."

It was Christi's turn to laugh. "I can still be a bit opinionated; just ask Dad. But I really want to be more like you and listen better."

"Molly, I so admire the unfailing love and devotion that you have as a mother. I'm amazed at how well you take care of Katie B. You show me how never to give up, no matter how great the challenge. Very few people would be able to love the way you love Katie."

"I saw that same selfless motherly love when you helped take care of my little girls when I had to go to Iraq. You and Dad were able to help Mom and Nathan take care of them and love them. My little girls formed such a close bond with you that you truly changed their lives forever."

Molly reached over, hugged her, and tearfully replied, "Christi, that special year we had with your girls was a gift from God. Thank you for sharing them with us."

Wiping tears from her eyes, Christi replied, "Thank you for loving them so dearly. Over the years, you have made so many wonderful things for my children and me. I was often blown away by your many creations, including cheerleading dolls for me and dresses for Alexis. After we lost Brianna, you made me that priceless Brianna memory blanket. You know how to do it all, and you do it exceedingly well. You will always be someone I will look up to forever. I love you, Molly!"

❄ ❄ ❄

Molly's son Andy and his wife joined us after Christmas to spend some special time with us. Andy had met Ariadna at his brother's wedding fifteen years ago. Maria and Ariadna were close friends who were both from Bogotá, Colombia. They went to the same college to study music. Ariadna often got up early and enjoyed talking with Molly before the boys filled the house with noise and activity.

"Molly, I want you to know that I treasure these times when we open our hearts and talk about God. You always amaze me with the way you so joyfully serve others," commented Ariadna early one morning.

"Well," Molly thoughtfully replied, "even though we do not belong to the same denomination, we're both Christians. It's okay to believe differently about a few things, like celebrating Christmas. I think I understand why you don't celebrate the holiday. What really matters is that we love the Lord and each other."

"Thank you, Molly," responded Ariadna, nodding her head. "I appreciate how respectful you are about my beliefs. That means so much to me. I see how you focus on the one most important thing we have in common, which is loving God and trying our best to please Him. I also admire the incredible and beautiful relationships you have with Maria's boys. It is a joy to see you spreading your love and joy to them and simply having so much fun with them, but always teaching them many things too. It is really beautiful to witness. Thank you for making me a part of your family!"

❄ ❄ ❄

DECEMBER 26—TIM'S JOURNAL ENTRY

Molly has suffered so much over the last six days. She is unable to hold any food down and keeps vomiting throughout the night. I was afraid she might have developed a tumor that has shut down the digestive system. Or the cancer may have moved into her esophagus or her stomach.

We went to see Molly's gastrointestinal specialist today. He believes Molly has a partial blockage in her intestines. The doctor says she may have a few days or weeks before she passes away. I am no longer shocked or dismayed by such bad news. I've come to accept the near certainty that my dear Molly will soon die. Unless the Lord grants her miraculous healing, she will soon be set free from her pitiful shrunken body and put an incredibly beautiful robe of righteousness on her brand-new body.

We're now beginning to talk about her celebration of life service and who will sing her favorite songs. She confided to me that she was considering recording a message of encouragement for family and friends. We both are coming to recognize that her time to go may be very near. We try to walk in faith, but sometimes our days are exceedingly difficult. People are always calling or coming by to love on her and encourage her. I want quiet times alone with Molly, but I know our friends and family need comfort too.

Indeed, this Christmas is a season to be born and probably a season to die. A season to rejoice and a season to cry. It is a sweet time being together with family, yet bitter because Molly is so sick. We all know this may be our last Christmas together, and if she passes away, everything will change forever. The delightful, warm family gatherings that we have enjoyed for so many decades may soon be just a fond memory.

Oh Lord, please give me the right words, a kind heart, and wisdom to care for Molly. Help me love her and everyone who comes to visit. I purpose to keep praising You, oh God, and desperately cling to Your promises. You alone have words of life.

*Bless the L*ORD*, O my soul; and all that is within me, bless His holy name! Bless the L*ORD*, O my soul, and forget not all His benefits: who forgives all your iniquities, who heals all your diseases, who redeems your life from destruction, who crowns you with lovingkindness and tender mercies. (Ps. 103:1–4 NKJV)*

18

TWENTY-FIVE WONDERFUL
YEARS TOGETHER

JANUARY 15, 2019

By the grace of God, we made it to our twenty-fifth wedding anniversary. I didn't know if Molly would still be with me on our special day. We were so thankful the Lord granted us more time so we could celebrate twenty-five wonderful years together. Our dear friend Russ Miller performed another home concert for a few special friends and us that morning. We had a delightful time worshiping the Lord, basking in His presence, and savoring everyone's love. One of Molly's spiritual daughters, Cristina McOmber, sang the beautiful and deeply moving song "Give Me Jesus." The presence of the Lord was alive in the room. His love washed over us like a warm Caribbean wave, and everybody cried. It was a truly unforgettable way to celebrate our anniversary with some of our very best friends.

Molly was doing great in spirit but very poorly in her body those days. She had been unable to hold down any solid food for the past three weeks. Her intestinal blockage continued to grow. She was eating very little and surviving on protein shakes. Molly had lost a great deal of muscle mass, and she was extremely weak and tired. But we thanked the Lord that He had answered our prayers to ease Molly's suffering. She was free from the horrible debilitating pain that so many people with cancer suffer. She treated her various aches and pains with essential oils and Tylenol.

Molly reminded me of John the Baptist. She was ever decreasing while the presence of the Lord was ever-increasing within her. Even though her body was wasting away, her spirit was shining brighter and brighter and touching so many lives. She was like a log of cherry wood burning bright on the hearth. As the log is consumed and disappears, it gives off a brilliant light, warmth, and such a sweet fragrance. Such was the glory of Molly's last days.

One day Janette, our hospice nurse, told me that Molly had only a few weeks left with us. Molly was still praying for her miracle but was ready and willing to go if it was God's will to take her home. She looked forward to being with her Lord and Savior, her precious Brianna, and many other dear family and friends who had already gone home to glory.

I spent my days choosing joy over depression. I tried to talk to the Lord about everything going on. I cried out for mercy and grace to be poured upon Molly and to fill us with joy and His presence. I refused to be critical and blame the Lord for Molly's cancer and this great trial. Instead, I meditated on scripture and gave thanks to the Lord for His great blessing in our lives. One of my favorites was from Thessalonians: *Rejoice always, pray without ceasing, in everything give thanks; for this is the will of God in Christ Jesus for you. (1 Thess. 5:16–18 NKJV).*

✳ ✳ ✳

We seldom talked about anything of substance. The cancer had robbed Molly's magnificent mind of energy, and she struggled to think clearly and communicate her heart. Molly must have sensed that her last days were drawing near, so she made an extraordinary effort to remind us of her love even after she was gone. She recorded wonderful audio messages for me, for my girls, for each of the older grandchildren, and for the memorial service. Each message was special, so warm and loving, so heart-wrenching. It was as though Molly were giving us a piece of herself so we could remember her forever.

MOLLY'S FAREWELL MESSAGE TO TIM

Oh, my dearest Tim,

Twenty-five years ago, I was totally overwhelmed that someone could love me and take me in, and take Katie in, and protect me and honor me, trust me, and just love me. I'm still overwhelmed.

We have had some difficult times, but we have not had anything as difficult as this. But in this season, we have learned to honor each other, and care for each other, and listen to each other, and love each other even more.

Tim, there's no way I can imagine my life without you. It's been just wonderful, adventurous, happy, adventurous; I said adventurous twice because I think that twice. Truly it's been a wonderful life together. It's a wonderful, wonderful life. I thank you, I thank you so much for all you've taught me, where you have brought me, for all you have cared for me. I love you more all the time because you are more and more loveable all the time as you become more like Christ. I see it in you, and I love you for it.

I know if I pass away first, and that's pretty likely, I'm going to be in a beautiful place, and you are going to be here, being more and more transformed by Him every day. I can't imagine trusting anybody else for Katie's future.

It is more than I can express what a wonderful person you are—that you are a man of faith and a man of integrity. That's always been so important to me: that you are a man of integrity.

I love you, Tim. I will be watching over you from heaven.

God bless you in Jesus' name.

Love, Molly

Listen carefully: Unless a grain of wheat is buried in the ground, dead to the world, it is never any more than a grain of wheat. But if it is buried, it sprouts and reproduces itself many times over. In the same way, anyone who holds on to life just as it is destroys that life. But if you let it go, reckless in your love, you'll have it forever, real and eternal. (John 12:24–25 NKJV)

19

ASLAN IS COMING

JANUARY 20, 2019

The stone-cold days of January were finally ending, and so was my hope for Molly. I slept alone since Molly never left her couch anymore. Sorrow and grief were my grim companions on the hard nights. Despite Molly still clinging to a thread of faith that God would save her, I was less hopeful, for Molly's days seemed very few.

Then the Lord encouraged us through an incredible experience. We had been reading an amazing book by Patti Callahan, *Becoming Mrs. Lewis.* It was a fictional account based very closely on the true story of C. S. Lewis and his marriage with Joy Davidman. It is a beautiful love story that fleshes out C. S. Lewis and the depth of his profound character. Patti revealed his love and devotion to Joy, a brilliant, gifted writer, and poet who was in great need. After many years of correspondence on the most profound issues of spirit and life, they became best friends and true soul mates.

At the end of the story, they discovered that Joy had terminal cancer, and the doctors sent her home to die. They struggled with issues of love and intimacy, pain and suffering, life and impending death, just as we were. We were deeply moved and shed many tears reading the ending of this heart-wrenching story.

Lewis repeatedly spoke of surrendering to the will of God and the plans of God. He, too, faced life without the one he loved more than any other, more than life itself. His love and the depth of his pain deeply impacted his writing. Out of profound grief, he shared his struggles, questions, and doubts.

We read the very end of the book on a Friday evening. Joy spoke about her attraction to lions and how she loved Aslan, C. S. Lewis's great lion of Narnia.

I said to Molly, "I hope that Aslan will come soon with Brianna riding on His shoulders to take you home for a new great adventure."

Molly shook her head and laughed. "You know, he's not a tame lion."

Nodding, I replied, "Yes, but he is *very good!*"

ASLAN—THE LION OF THE TRIBE OF JUDAH

Rhema Peet was one of our dear young friends in the church. She shares her story about Aslan and Molly.

"Our family began attending Our Father's House in 2010. Molly quickly stood out to me as someone I wanted to know and emulate. I gleaned from her experiences and insights in our women's Bible studies. I watched how she grieved the loss of Brianna, her precious granddaughter, and of course, her loving commitment and care for Katie B. I enjoyed Molly's down-to-earth humor as we picnicked with our family small-group. She always had thoughtful questions to ask and an ability to express understanding and care. My most precious memory of Molly was when I accompanied her to her neighbor's infrared sauna for her cancer treatment. I felt like a trusted daughter as Molly, all skin and bones, sat with me. We were quiet for some minutes. Other minutes she would pray, thanking God for her family, for who He is. She asked Him to help her and heal her. We talked of her saying good-bye to Tim and other sacred things. It was holy ground."

"As Molly declined in January of 2019, I began to sense that I should paint something for her—but what? We all knew that she would only be with us a matter of weeks, barring a miracle. How would a painting that she would soon leave behind be a good gift? I wrestled with the idea and felt afraid to bring harm by missing the mark. Still, the feeling stirred inside me to the point that I couldn't resist it."

"I set up my painting supplies on the kitchen table and closed my eyes, praying, '*Lord, please show me what I should paint for Molly.*' Immediately, a picture of a lion popped into my head. And so, I painted 'Molly's Lion.' I listened to worship music while I worked. A song popped out to me, and I knew it was significant, perhaps a message for Molly. The words, 'I am not alone; You will go before me; You will never leave me,' rang true. I wrote her a card, put the finished lion in a bag, and dropped it off at the Frinks' on Saturday morning."

"A few hours later, I received the most unexpected phone call of my life."

I AM NOT ALONE

When we opened Rhema's gift later that day, we were astounded to see that she had painted a beautiful watercolor of a lion. It was Aslan—the Lion of the tribe of Judah. Her card read, "This painting was inspired by Carrie Jobe's song 'I Am Not Alone,' which had words that I thought were so appropriate for you: 'I am not alone; I am not alone; You will go before me; You'll never leave me.'"

The Spirit of the Lord absolutely overwhelmed us and filled us with joy and thanksgiving as we beheld the Lion of the tribe of Judah in all His glory. He was speaking right to our hearts, directly into our lives, in a divine confirmation of what we'd read the day before. He is such a good, good God. We knew no matter what lay ahead on this painful journey, Jesus, the Lion of Judah, had just assured us He would walk beside us every step of the way. He would carry Molly home.

Some people might think we were depressed, experiencing a terrible tragedy. However, we considered ourselves blessed, for we knew that God is the rewarder of those who diligently seek and follow Him. Molly would soon receive the reward she richly deserved. We saw His glory shining in so many powerful ways as we continued to share the love of God with our family and friends. No matter what the world might offer, we said, "Give me Jesus." No matter what would happen, we knew that it was all about His love. And if Molly would soon go home to be with Jesus, He would receive all the glory and all the honor, for He alone was worthy, worthy, worthy of all our praise.

But without faith, it is impossible to please Him, for he who comes to God must believe that He is, and that He is a rewarder of those who diligently seek Him. (Heb. 11:6 NKJV)

20

ALMOST HOME

*B*y the beginning of February, it had been over six weeks since Molly took a turn for the worse and stopped eating. She was barely surviving on a liquid diet of fewer than 150 calories a day. Molly had lost almost fifty pounds, was emaciated, and looked like a victim from a concentration camp. She was so weak she could not walk, slept most of the time, and seldom talked anymore. Most nights were very hard for her. She had begun having serious pain in her abdomen and excruciating chest spasms, making it very difficult to breathe.

Molly's final weeks were very hard for all of us, with a few good days and many bad nights. She was not getting better but was slowly, very slowly, dying before my eyes. We kept climbing the high, hard, cold mountains. Some days we thought she might be getting a bit better, but there was always another daunting mountain ahead. We struggled through deep ravines of pain, yet pressed upward under the very shadow of death. We clung to the Good Shepherd's rod and His staff and leaned on Him as never before on our journey to the high places.

Molly needed assistance to do everything. Since she was too weak to walk, I carried her, lifting her under her arms so she could tiptoe to the bathroom.

One time as we shuffled down the hall, she remarked, "It's so easy to walk when you lift me in your arms. I feel like I'm walking on air."

"When you are weak, I am strong," I replied.

At that moment, the Lord spoke to me. I heard His still quiet voice in my mind, "*As you are carrying Molly, I am carrying both of you, for I am very strong!*"

I immediately remembered the Scripture in Isaiah that Molly had shared with our waitress Sue and was greatly encouraged: "*Fear not for I am with you. Do not be dismayed, for I am your God. I will strengthen you, yes I will help you, I will uphold you with My righteous right hand*" (*Isa. 41:10 NKJV*).

❄ ❄ ❄

I often felt lost at sea in a bone-chilling, gloomy fog with no breeze to carry us home. I wanted Molly to be healed and never leave me, but I also wanted her terrible suffering to end. I remembered a great quote I read somewhere: "Uncertainty is the cross God always gives us in this life." I craved certainty, will Molly live or soon die? But I had to patiently wait on the Lord for His will to be done. **Nevertheless, not My will. But your will be done. (Luke 22:42)**

One night I got up to check on Molly. Her suffering was breaking my heart. She still was refusing opioids because she hated how they made her feel. She only wanted Tylenol and having me rub her belly, skeletal chest, and back with pain-relieving essential oils.

As I massaged her skin and bones, she quietly moaned while tears fell from my eyes. "I don't fear death; I fear living any longer if I keep having such pain and these terrible nights."

Many times throughout these very hard days, I cried out, "Oh Lord, please either take my poor, suffering Molly home soon or grant her Your miraculous healing. Please, Jesus, we are so desperate. Please help us!"

TIM'S JOURNAL ENTRY FOR FEBRUARY 6

It breaks my heart to sit here and watch you slowly die. I can't help you when you choke and can't breathe due to chest spasms. I feel so helpless, so hopeless. You are suffering so much physically while I'm hurting so much emotionally.

I struggle to believe and keep on giving, while you struggle to breathe and keep on living.

I can't bear the thought of losing you, my best friend, my forever soul mate. The beautiful threads of your life have been woven like needlepoint through the fabric of my being. The tapestry of my soul reflects your amazing love.

Some people say we are so strong, but I feel so weak and desperate for mercy and grace in our time of great need. Lord, how long, how long will You continue to let her live and suffer? I surrender my broken heart to You. I surrender Molly to You. Please take her home very soon. The good-byes have been said, the videos recorded, the tears shed. Yet she continues to live on, a mere shadow of her magnificent life. I wait on you "for Your compassions never fail. They are new every morning. Great is your faithfulness." Please, please, Lord, set her free. Please take her home.

ALMOST HOME

Friday, February 8

I finally convinced Molly to let us move a hospital bed into the living room so she could rest more comfortably. We could also take care of her far better. Molly finally agreed to start taking Lorazepam and OxyContin to ease the increasing pain and help her sleep. On Friday, she was so drugged and weak she could hardly speak to us. We wondered if she had finally come to an end, but she rallied a bit on Saturday morning and gave us two requests: "Please embrace, please smile."

Hour by hour, she was barely responsive and unable to talk. Our closest friends visited us for the next two days to keep her company.

Pastor Lanny and Pastor Jay came to support us with their love and prayers. Pastor Lanny had been Molly's spiritual father for the last thirty-five years. Molly had the utmost admiration, respect, and love for Lanny.

Molly had been a spiritual mother to Jay ever since he and his wife, Katie, joined our church right after college fourteen years earlier. Jay pulled a chair close to Molly, held her hand, and shared his heart with her.

"Molly, I've always been so impressed by the way you love the Lord and the way you love people. You have such an intimacy with Him and trust in Him. You know that He will provide whatever you need. Your faith has always amazed me.

"I remember your story about often misplacing your car keys and how you would ask the Lord for guidance. He always showed you where the keys were. You knew that He cared about all the little things in your life. You were always sharing about your experiences and His responses in situations like these. I know God delights in you, and you showed me how I can delight in Him.

"The message of your life that has spoken the loudest to me is how you've chosen to live out your last days. I admire your commitment to the Lord to live in expectancy rather than having expectations of what He should do for you. My paradigm has shifted as I have watched you live out this profound understanding. You experience Him in ways I cannot imagine. He obviously is sustaining you and pouring out His love through you to everyone who has come to visit. Even though you are so weak, you chose to minister to all who came to minister to you and showed genuine love and care for everyone. I am grateful for your example, and I'm so thankful for the way you loved me. You have left an incredible legacy. I love you."

Tears ran down his face, and Jay bent over Molly to hug her and kiss her good-bye. Pastor Lanny and Pastor Jay then laid hands on Molly and prayed for her one last time.

LAST DAYS

The weekend had been emotionally exhausting for me, with so many people wanting to talk to us and pray. We were all grieving, expecting Molly would soon pass away. I was relieved when the last friend left late Sunday night, so I could finally go to bed.

As I bent over Molly to bless her and say good night, I softly said, "Please give me a good kiss; it might be our very last."

She opened her eyes, mustered her strength, and indignantly whispered, "So, you *have* finally given up on me!"

Surprised and taken aback at her accusation, I shook my head. "No, no, no! I haven't given up on you. The cancer has won; your body is giving up. Unless the Lord raises you up, like Lazarus, it sure looks like you're going home very soon."

She looked so sad and did not reply. She closed her eyes, turned her head, and refused to kiss me good night. After fighting so valiantly for six long, hard months, she seemed to finally accept her fate. Disheartened, I went to bed completely broken and cried myself to sleep.

Monday morning, I was surprised Molly was still alive, though barely responsive. Janette, our faithful hospice nurse, came over to examine her. She said Molly's pulse was rapid, and her blood pressure was very shallow. Janette believed Molly only had a day or two left. She encouraged Molly to say her good-byes since her time was very short. Molly took the news with surprising acceptance. She had finally come to the point where she was willing to die and go home. She seemed to say, "Nevertheless, not my will, but Your will, Lord, be done."

But then Molly amazed all of us and rallied with renewed energy. She spent hours listening to final words and sharing a word or two with our kids and her family. A small group of our closest friends came over to be with her for the day. We had an extraordinary experience later that afternoon when we thought she was finally going home.

After anointing Katie and praying for her, suddenly Molly opened her eyes wide and, with a surge of energy, announced, "Look, I see Brianna, I see Aslan, I see Jesus!"

She hugged me and said good-bye to everyone with great passion. We all cried and sang and prayed and worshiped. We were confident that at any moment, Molly would close her eyes and be gone. We continued worshiping and praying, but for some reason, she stayed with us. After a few hours of worship and prayer, Molly was quite disappointed that the Lord hadn't taken her home when He visited her. She then slipped into a semi-comatose state and was unresponsive for the rest of the day.

On Tuesday, Janette said Molly's pulse was very shallow and rapid, and her blood pressure was undetectable. She had finally come to the end of her hard, painful journey. Molly spent the rest of the day slowly slipping away, hardly able to speak but still recognizing those visiting. At one point, she whispered so softly we had to strain to hear her: "I am afraid." I gently embraced her, tears coursing down my cheeks, and comforted her. We prayed for the peace that passes all understanding to come upon her. And Jesus, the Prince of Peace, touched her soul and took away her fear. An ever so small smile touched her lips, and she fell into a deep sleep.

As I watched Molly slowly heading home, I remembered a passage from her testimony:

I know that God is with me. He's going to give me grace and comfort as He always has. He's there all the time. He's going to lead my family if they have to handle my passing on to heaven. I'll be in His presence, and they will be here taking care of each other. And He's going to lead them. But my expectancy is that He will heal me and lead me as I rejoin them as a wife and a mother instead of someone who is dependent and needs a caretaker. I surrender all that to You, Lord. I just give up. I give up. I wave the white flag. I accept whatever You have for me.

For this light momentary affliction is preparing for us an eternal weight of glory beyond all comparison. (2 Cor. 4:17 ESV)

21

AMAZING GRACE

FEBRUARY 13, 2019

After a long, emotionally draining day, I fully expected Molly to pass away while I slept. She had been so close to slipping into eternity all day long. She had always wanted me to be with her at the very end, but I had no idea how to make that happen. I couldn't stay with her every moment, day and night.

So I kissed her good night one last time and told her, "Dear Molly, you can go home tonight; just let go and let Jesus take you home." I went to sleep listening to her very slow, quiet breathing on the baby monitor.

Over those last several months, we had shared many extraordinary moments around 3:00 a.m. Many a night, I comforted Molly when she couldn't sleep, for she was in such great discomfort and pain. While I massaged her shrunken, broken body, we would watch the fire and talk until I would start falling asleep, and she would send me back to bed. Those were such precious moments of intimacy, moments of light in great darkness.

I woke again at 3:00 a.m., and I wondered if Molly was still alive since I couldn't hear her on the monitor. I found her ever so quiet, barely breathing.

I sat close beside her and held her hand, and started talking to her. "Molly, I love you. I will love you till the end of time. I will never forget how you opened your heart and loved me when I was so fragile, so broken. Your life was full, and you never expected to marry again. I know you were looking forward to a quiet, peaceful life with Katie B. with the boys in college. Yet, you were willing to love me and my hurting girls and blend my broken family with yours. You showed us such grace and mercy. I promise I will do my best to take care of our family and keep us together. I will find a good home for our precious Katie B., I promise."

I spent a long time talking to her, reminiscing about our twenty-five wonderful years together. We had shared the best of times; we suffered through some of the very worst times. While I talked, Molly's breath was labored, so shallow, so soft.

I reminded her, "Molly, you are not alone; you are not alone; Jesus has prepared a new home for you. He will never forsake you; Jesus is here with you. He's ready to walk you home."

I then climbed into the hospital bed with her, and one last time I wrapped her in my arms. I told her all the things I was planning on sharing at her celebration of life service. I would tell her life story of how her great love had touched so many lives and triumphed over so much adversity.

With a breaking voice and tears freely flowing, I started singing her favorite worship songs that I had been singing those many weeks while rubbing her feet:

> *You are here*
> > *Moving in our midst*
> *I worship you; I worship you.*
> *Way maker, miracle worker,*
> > *promise keeper, light in the darkness,*
> *My God, that is who you are.*
>
> —"Waymaker" by Sinach

And I sang "Give me Jesus" by Fernando Ortega:

And when I am alone
Oh, and when I am alone
And when I am alone, give me Jesus

Give me Jesus
Give me Jesus
You can have all this world
But give me Jesus

And when I come to die
Oh, and when I come to die
And when I come to die, give me Jesus.

Time seemed to stretch to eternity with long pauses between each quiet breath. I held her ever so tight, pressing my ear to her chest. I could barely hear her heart as it beat slowly, ever so slowly. I wept in the awesome wonder of it all. My God was giving me the honor and incredible privilege to hold her in my arms as she left her broken body and walked into His arms. I then sensed the presence of the Holy Spirit envelop us. I had goosebumps on my arms. I could barely breathe. Time stood still.

Through the tears and overwhelming emotion, I was barely able to sing her favorite hymn, "Amazing Grace":

Amazing grace! How sweet the sound
That saved a wretch like me!
I once was lost, but now am found;
Was blind, but now I see.

'Twas grace that taught my heart to fear,
And grace my fears relieved;
How precious did that grace appear
The hour I first believed.

Through many dangers, toils, and snares,
I have already come;
'Tis grace hath brought me safe thus far,
And grace will lead me home.

As I sang the last verse, incredibly, Molly stopped breathing. I pressed my ear to her chest and heard her last heartbeat. Slowly but surely, her amazing, grace-filled heart finally rested in everlasting peace.

Overwhelmed with emotion, I sobbed, great grief mixed with tears of relief that her terrible battle was finally over. I loudly cried out: "My Molly, my dear Molly, you're gone, forever gone. You always told me that you wanted me to be with you at the very end. That is why you held out for so long. You waited for a still, quiet hour when we were all alone, and I could embrace you and tell you one last time, 'I love you.'"

"Farewell, my beloved. I'm not saying good-bye, but until we meet again. I will love you forever. You are alive! You are alive! Heaven's gates are thrown open wide!"

And Jesus replied, "I assure you, today you will be with me in paradise." (Luke 23:43 NKJV)

22

EPILOGUE –
IT'S ALL ABOUT LOVE!

*I*had always been so impressed by Molly's sincere devotion to following Jesus, the living God of the universe. Though her path was very hard at times, as a Christ-follower, Molly richly deserved to be with Him forevermore. Hanna Hurnard, in her classic *Hinds' Feet on High Places,* summed up Molly's life so well:

"The secret of experiencing true love is to go lower.
Pour yourself down.
Go lower and lower.
Give and give and give,
and serve with joyful abandonment."

I am so proud of the way that Molly loved everyone in her straightforward, simple way. She considered herself just an ordinary woman who willingly gave herself for everyone the Lord brought into her life. I sincerely hope that all of her family and friends will strive to live the theme song of her life; "It Is All About Love."

Over the decades, Molly had spent countless hours with the Lord in prayer, worship, and in His Word. Walking in His presence day by day had given her an intimate, abiding relationship with Jesus. She had such an expectancy that Jesus had a unique plan for her even in the greatest crisis of her life. Molly abandoned herself and waved the white flag of surrender to the Lord and His purposes for her. She lay down her life moment by moment, day by day, to one and all. Molly knew that God permits what He hates in order to accomplish what He loves.

The battle rages on as storm and tempest roar
We cannot win this fight against cancer, Lord
We're laying down our weapons now.

She raised her white flag
She surrendered all to You, all to You.
She raised her white flag.

The war is over. Love has come. Your love has won.
Here on this holy ground, You made a way for her peace.
"White Flag" by Chris Tomlin
(with the lyrics slightly modified to reflect Molly's journey home)

Hilton Garcia, a friend in our church, had recently passed away. Knowing he would soon die due to a severely damaged heart, Hilton recorded a deeply moving message that his family played at his memorial service.

Molly really liked what Hilton had done. It was so moving, so powerful. So she recorded her own final words of encouragement to be shared at her memorial service just in case the Lord decided not to heal her:

"If you are watching this video of my life at my celebration of life service, I am in heaven with Jesus watching you. I've been battling this cancer now for six months, and I have had the opportunity to spend time with many of you, encouraging you to surrender your life to

Christ. If you do that, you will find the love and the peace that I have. You can have all this world, but give me Jesus!

"I want to say to all of you how blessed I am to have had you in my life. I thank you for carrying me through this very difficult trial. Tim, Katie B., and Caitlin have been my full-time love and support. So many family members and dear friends have called me, visited me, and loved me so deeply. Other friends have sung songs over me, played music for me, brought me flowers, taken me to the infrared sauna, made so many wonderful meals, and even cleaned out the basement and closets throughout my house. I am so rich in my relationships because Jesus came and showed us how to love as He does. It's truly all about love.

"I will forever cherish this amazing family that I have, my dear mom and dad, who built such a great foundation of values in my life. I love my dear siblings and their spouses, Ron and Joanne, Barb and Tom, Dave and Lena, and Mark and Janet. I am exceedingly blessed above and beyond measure by my five wonderful children and their spouses and my nine grandchildren that God has given me: Andy and Ariadna, Nate and Maria, Carlo, Paolo, and Matteo, Katie B., Katie and Kyle, Zebulon, and Ezra, Christi, and Christopher, Brianna, Alexis, Caylee, and Jaynee. Beyond these beloved ones, I have such amazing nieces and nephews.

"Now I have passed through this kingdom on earth, and I have ascended into my Father's house in heaven. I love you all, and I want to see you again. Most of you who are watching know the way to get here, but some of you may be unsure or working hard to earn your heavenly reward. And some of you are lost, wondering what will happen to you when you die. You may believe in God, pray, and even go to church, just trying to live a virtuous life. Those are all good, but unless they lead to a relationship with Jesus, they have no effect. Jesus came in the form of a man to teach us how to be reconciled with our Father God and be a part of His family. Do you know what Jesus said? *'I am the way, the truth, and the life. No one can come to the Father except through Me.'*

"I was thirty-six-years old and living a life apart from God and doing my own thing. Then, in a moment of crisis, Jesus responded to my desperation, set me free from my sins, and welcomed me into the family of God. Now I am recording this message while still on the earth, just like you. But I know already that I am in His kingdom, assured of His love for me, ready to pass from this earth into my new heavenly home and join my precious Brianna and other dear family and friends who have gone on ahead of me.

"Jesus loved me and gave His life for me while I was a sinner and didn't know Him at all. For God so loved the world—that means all of you—that He gave his only begotten Son, Jesus, that whoever believes in Him would not perish, but have everlasting life.

"Please, you have nothing to lose and everything to gain by pursuing a relationship with Jesus Christ. If you have any doubts, ask the Lord if He is real, and He will reveal Himself to you. There are no risks. There are no side effects, and there are no unintended consequences; all you need to do is surrender to Him and receive His love. He loves you just as He loves me. Jesus is the man who is all about love. He is waiting for you to surrender and follow Him.

"I love all of you, goodbye."

Greater love has no one than this: to lay down one's life for one's friends. (John 15:13 NIV)